Early Indiana Trails and Surveys

By George R. Wilson, C.E., L.L.B.

Ex-County Surveyor of Dubois County; and Author of
History of Dubois County

D1166678

[1919]

Indiana Historical Society
1986

First Edition 1919
(Indianapolis: Indiana Historical Society Publications,
Vol. 6, No. 3, 1919)

Reprinted 1972 by
The Society of Indiana Pioneers
By arrangement with the Indiana Historical Society

Library of Congress Cataloging in Publication Data

Wilson, George R., 1863-1941.
  Early Indiana trails and surveys.

  Reprint. Originally published: 1919. (Indiana
Historical Society publications; v. 6, no. 3)
  Includes bibliographical references and index.

  1. Trails—Indiana.   2. Indian trails—Indiana.
3. Indiana—Surveys.   I. Indiana Historical Society.
II. Title.   III. Series: Indiana Historical Society
publications; v. 6, no. 3.
F521.I41   vol. 6, no. 3 1986   917.72'043   86-10430
[F526]

Early Indiana Trails and Surveys

PART I.

EARLY TRAILS.

The most prominent early line of travel on land in southern Indiana was the *Buffalo Trace,* also called the "Kentucky Road," "Vincennes Trace," "Clarksville Trace," "Harrison's Road," "Lan-an-zo-ki-mi-wi," etc. It entered Indiana at the Falls of the Ohio, passed in a northwesterly direction and left Indiana at Vincennes. As a line of travel between the same two points, this old trail was as prominent in 1800 and previous thereto as the Baltimore & Ohio Railroad is to-day. The buffaloes passed over it in great numbers, and kept it open, in many places twenty feet wide. It was a beaten and well worn path, so prominent and conspicuous that, in 1804, it was used by General Harrison and the Indians to locate a treaty line.[1] Forty-three miles of it, from "Clark's Grant" to the east line of the Vincennes Tract, in Orange county, were surveyed by "calls," that is, by courses and distances, by Surveyor William Rector, in August,[2] 1805. His survey was

1

[1] Indiana Historical Society's Publication 4, pp. 254, 255, 383, 312, 190 and 256; same, Volume 2, p. 16; same, Volume 2, p. 464; Miscellaneous Record 1, pp. 29, 33, 37 and 39, State Auditor's Office; Smith's *Indiana,* Volume 1, pp. 232 and 233; Glasscock's *Indiana,* pp. 155-162; Indiana Plat Book 5, pp. 6, 12 and 24; Record 5, N. & W., p. 242; Record 4, N. & W., p. 190; Record 3, N. & W., p. 173; Record 1, N. & W. p. 4.

[2] Miscellaneous Record 1, *Indiana,* State Auditor's Office, p. 37; see Record of Survey 31, of Clark's Grant, made in 1785, in Clark county, land now owned by Sheriff Isaac R. Phipps.

made in order to run the north line of the Vincennes treaty concession of 1804. The remaining part, as well as the part surveyed by Mr. Rector may be exactly determined by reference to the field notes of the deputy surveyors who subdivided the Vincennes Tract and the Vincennes treaty concessions, in 1804-5. The records are part of the land department of the State Auditor's Office. The old trace follows the Buckingham base line very closely, through Dubois and Pike counties, and crosses White river on its way to Vincennes six miles west of the confluence of its two forks. N. Harlan's ferry had been established there previous[3] to 1805. It is likely that Abraham Lincoln crossed White river at this ferry, in 1830, on his way from Spencer county, Indiana, to Illinois.

The southwest boundary of what afterward became known as the "New Purchase" is often called the "ten o'clock line." In making the survey of the "ten o'clock line" from the mouth of Raccoon creek to Jackson county, John McDonald, the surveyor crossed several Indian traces or lines of travel. He made the survey in 1810. The line is more than 94 miles in length. Near what is now Bridgeton, he recorded an Indian trail going southwest, or northeast.[4] He also recorded an

[3] Record 9, pp. 403, 411 and 425, N. & W., Land Department State Auditor's Office; Indiana Historical Society's Publication 2, pp. 366 and 458, and Volume 3, p. 97; Plat Book 5, pp. 27 and 157; Record N. & W. 6, p. 246; Record N. & W. 5, p. 242; Record N. & W. 5, pp. 5, 12 and 24; Record N. & W. 1, p. 4; Record N. & W. 4, p. 190; Record N. & W. 3, pp. 141 to 173; Wilson's *History of Dubois County*, p. 28; Esarey's *Indiana*, pp. 38 and 144; for map see Smith's *Indiana*; American State Papers, Class 2, *Indian Affairs*, pp. 689 and 690; Senate Documents, Volume 39, pp. 70, 71 and 72; Indiana Historical Society's Publication 2, pp. 366 and 464; Cockrum's *Pioneer History of Indiana*, p. 490.

[4] Dillon's *Indiana*, p. 447; Esarey's *Indiana*, pp. 210 and 229; Miscellaneous Record 1, *Indiana*, pp. 73 and 89.

Indian road at what is now Gosport ,and one between Cataract and Santa Fe. Ten miles east of Bloomington he crossed an Indian trail running north and south.[5] South of White river, near Brownstown, he recorded another Indian road, going east and west[6]; west perhaps to the old Delaware camp at the forks of White river. There was an army crossing at the mouth of Raccoon creek;[7] the trail crossed the Wabash there and followed up the right hand or west bank of the river. This fact made the mouth of Raccoon creek prominent enough to be a beginning point of the "Harrison Purchase,"[8] in 1809. On this "ten o'clock line" there was an Indian trail between what is now Dana and Hillsdale.[9] Since the line ran in a southeasterly direction, the traces must have crossed it nearly at right angles, or the surveyor would not have recorded them. Probably all led toward Ft. Wayne and Vincennes.[10] The survey of this line was not pleasing to Tecumseh, and he so intimated to the United States government, August 10, 1810, at Vincennes.[11] He was very angry at the chiefs who "touched the quill," as the Indians called signing a treaty.

3

[5] Miscellaneous Record 1, *Indiana,* pp. 90 and 101.

[6] Miscellaneous Record 1, *Indiana,* p. 115; Record N. & W. 2, p. 420; Plat Book 2, p. 17, State Auditor's Office; Cockrum's *Pioneer History of Indiana,* p. 373.

[7] Indiana Historical Society's Publication 4, pp. 277 and 180; Cockrum's *Pioneer History of Indiana,* pp. 242 and 258; *Centennial History and Handbook of Indiana,* pp. 45 and 59; Dillon's *Indiana,* p. 447; Esarey's *Indiana,* pp. 38 and 65; *History of Indiana,* by Goodrich & Tuttle, p. 155.

[8] Manuscript No. 49062 Indiana State Library, pp. 71, 72, 73 and 74; Dillon's *Indiana,* pp. 535-538; Senate Documents Volume 39, pp. 101 and 102; American State Papers, Class 2, *Indian Affairs,* p. 761.

[9] Miscellaneous Record 1, *Indiana,* p. 119; Cockrum's *Pioneer History of Indiana,* p. 63.

[10] Esarey's *Indiana,* pp. 246 and 345.

[11] Dillon's *Indiana,* pp. 431 and 454.

At the mouth of the Kentucky river, and on its right hand bank stood "Fort William,"[12] in 1805. It is now Carrolton, Kentucky. This was a point on the Greenville Treaty line.[13]

An Indian trail which passed through the "gore," crossed the Greenville Treaty line about 71 miles from the Ohio river.[14] This old trail was a short distance north of Liberty, Indiana, and may have led to Liberty. It was indicated as an "Indian road to White river," by John Brownson,[15] the surveyor, in 1806. It may have led to "Shield's Trading House," near Seymour.

There were early trails running east and west through Dearborn county. One went from near Milan toward Cincinnati. The survey records call it "Kibbey's Road."[16] It was the first one crossing the entire state from Cincinnati to Vincennes, and was laid out early in the nineteenth century, perhaps in 1801-2. The *Western Spy,* published in Cincinnati July 23, 1799, contained the following item: "Captain E. Kibbey, who some time since undertook to cut a road from Vincennes to this place, returned on Monday, reduced to a perfect skeleton. He had cut the road 70 miles, when, by some means, he was separated from his men. After hunting them some days without success, he steered his course this way. He had undergone great hardships and was obliged to

---

[12] Plat Book 1, pp. 71-108.

[13] Volume 3, W. of 1st Mer., p. 96.

[14] Plat Book 1, p. 15.

[15] Plat Book 1, p. 17; Cockrum's *Pioneer History of Indiana,* p. 102.

[16] Plat Book 1, pp. 39-45; Samuel McCoy's novel *"Tippecanoe,"* p. 152; Indiana Historical Society's Publications, Volume 1, pp. 256, 259, 260, 279, 292, 340, 341 and 347; *Notes on a Journey in America,* 1818, by Morris Birkbeck. pp. 78-89; Brown's *Western Gazetteer,* p. 79.

subsist upon roots, etc., which he picked up in the woods." Twenty years later gazetteers described the line of the road west from Cincinnati as "Burlington, 15 miles; Rising Sun, 10; Judge Cotton's, 20; Madison, 20; New Lexington, 17; Salem, 32; French Lick, 34; east fork White river, 17; north fork White river, 20; Vincennes, 16; total, 201 miles."

The other road passed a mile south of Chesterville, just north of Aurora, and probably through what is now Lawrenceburg to Cincinnati. One may have led from *"Shield's Trading House,"* at Seymour, and the other one from near French Lick to Cincinnati. Thomas Freeman, the Vincennes tract surveyor, in 1802, records a 'trace to Cincinnati," about thirteen miles south of Orleans, in Orange county.[17] This may have been Captain Kibbey's road, and if so, it was the Kibbeys' road that crossed Salt creek and eventually became the north fork of the famous Vincennes and Clarksville trace, often called the Buffalo trace.

5

Prior to 1820, a store, or trading post was established at Hindostan, probably on Captain Kibbey's road, by Lewis Brooks, and from this store supplies for hunters, pioneers, etc., were taken down White river on boats to Portersville, the first "county town" of Dubois county. It was two miles from Portersville to the Buffalo trace, thus this plan connected the two forks of this road and furnished a connecting link in event of Indian trouble. Thomas J. Brooks conducted the store at Portersville. The tradition is that the Brooks bought their goods "on east," i. e., Cincinnati. They were Yankees

17 Brown's *Western Gazetteer*, pp. 62 and 63; Miscellaneous Record 1, *Indiana*, p. 29; Volume 3 *W. of First Meridian*, p. 96; 1800 State Auditor's Office; Plat Book 5, p. 136; Plat Book 1. page 127; *Early Travels in Indiana*, p. 232.

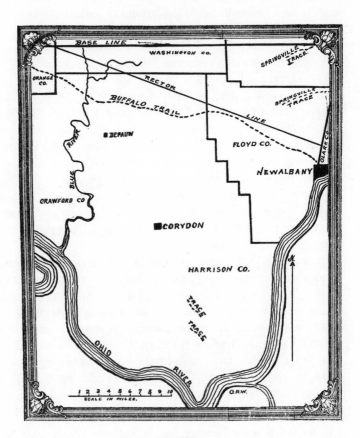

PLATE I.

and came from Concord, Massachusetts. Hindostan failed during the pestilence in Indiana between 1820 and 1822.[18]

An Indian trail led from Vallonia southeast through Washington and Scott counties into "Clark's Grant," entering it near the Pigeon Roost Monument, and probably going to the "Falls of the Ohio," by way of the old town of Springville, to which town two traces came from the west.[19] In 1801, Springville was the county seat of Clark county. Its history covered two years. It is now a ploughed field. Springville was situated on Pleasant Run, on the line between lots 94 and 115 in "Clark's Grant." It was a short distance from Charlestown.

Springville, like many other pioneer "county towns," has passed away, except upon the old maps and surveys, nevertheless, for this place on April 7, 1801, the first court of justice of the territory of Indiana was commissioned by General Harrison.

Springville was headquarters for those opposed to slavery in Indiana, in 1807. One trail from the west was about nine miles north of New Albany. It left Floyd county at its northeast corner, and entered Clark's Grant almost at the northeast corner of section 26, town 1 south, range 6 east. The other was thirteen miles north, and entered Clark's Grant one-half mile south of the base line, about half way between the base

7

[18] *Early Travels in Indiana*, pp. 178, 179 and 190; *Indiana Gazetteer*, pp. 118 and 119; Mrs. Eugenia C. Chappell, R. F. D. No. 2, Petersburg, Indiana, 1916; Dillon's *Indiana*, p. 522; Hindostan, a Pioneer Town, *Indiana Magazine of History*, June, 1914; Esarey's *Indiana*, pp. 239, 247, 254, 261, 355 and 370.

[19] Plat Book 5, pp. 195 and 198; Dillon's *Indiana*, pp. 412 and 492; Indiana Historical Society's Publication, Volume 2, pp. 128-134 and 518; Volume 3, p. 97; Smith's *Indiana*, p. 133; *History of Indiana* by Goodrich & Tuttle, p. 164; Morris Birkbeck's Notes, 1818, p. 83, *Sholt's Tavern*.

line and the Muddy fork of Silver creek. Springville had a stockade.[20]

In 1819, Surveyor B. F. Morris, in his survey of the land around Columbus, Indiana, recorded the east fork of White river under the name "Driftwood."[21]

Before the treaty of Vincennes, which gave the United States a title to the land between the Vincennes tract and the Ohio river, many persons who had started from Virginia, Tennessee, and the Carolinas, intending to settle in the Northwest Territory, had stopped in Kentucky, all along the southern bank of the Ohio river, and were waiting for an opportunity to enter Indiana, as soon as the government had possession and the surveys began. There is no regular survey in Kentucky, and settlers were never sure of their titles. Frequently all their possessions were lost through an unknown previous title or claim.

After the treaty these people entered Indiana over the Blue river, Rome, Yellow Banks, Red Banks, Saline, and other trails.[22] It is said that from 1785 to 1812 more than 2,000 men, women and children were carried into captivity from Kentucky and the Northwest Territory, and that not one in ten was ever heard of again.[23]

8

20 Brown's *Western Gazateer*, pp. 62 and 63; Indiana Historical Society's Publications, Vol. 2, p. 518, Vol. 3, pp. 97, 102; Dillon's *Indiana*, p. 412; See *"Illinois Grant,"* State Auditor's Office; Indianapolis News, June 9, 1915; Cockrum's *Pioneer History of Indiana*, p. 136; Dillon's *Indiana*, p. 203; Plat Book 5 p. 133; *Executive Journal Indiana Territory*, pp. 4, 109.

21 Plat Book 2, page 161; *Early Travels in Indiana*, pp. 138, 219; Brown's *"Western Gazetteer,"* pp. 39 and 40.

22 Dillon's *Indiana*, pp. 96 and 427; *American Archives*, 4th Series, Vol. 1, p. 1014; Holland's *Life of Lincoln*, pp. 25 and 26; Cockrum's *Pioneer History of Indiana*, pp. 150, 155, 200 and 243; Esarey's *History of Indiana*, p. 92.

23 Esarey's *History of Indiana*, pp. 160 and 168.

The surveyor of range 4 east, made a note of an Indian trace in Harrison county. A trace crossed the south fork of Buck creek two miles above its mouth. It is also recorded about two miles farther south. Probably this trace led from the Ohio river to Corydon, and eventually to the Buffalo trace, the main trunk line, so far as Indian traces, in southern Indiana, are concerned. Incidentally, the War of 1812 was the cause of the capital of Indiana Territory being moved from Vincennes to Corydon.[24] The Buffalo trace crossed Blue river two or three miles east of the southeast corner of Orange county. The Blue river crossing was historically prominent.[25] Squire Boone's mill stood on Buck creek, and Boone's "cave-sepulcher" is near by. The Buck creek trace was well known in the pioneer days of Harrison county.

There was a small fort on the Kentucky side of the Ohio, at the mouth of Salt river, and many pioneers came to Indiana, by way of this stream.[26]

There appears to have been an Indian trail five miles south of what is now Leopold, in Perry county. It led northwest from the Ohio river.[27] Going almost northwest from Rome, in Perry county, and leaving Cannelton, Tell City and Troy from six to eight miles south, an Indian road crossed the Anderson river three miles southeast of Fulda, passed through

9

[24] Samuel McCoy's novel, *"Tippecanoe,"* pp. 9 and 146; Cockrum's *Pioneer History of Indiana,* pp. 368 and 369; (Read General Gibson's speech).

[25] See Act creating Clark county; Miscellaneous Record Indiana, p. 37, State Auditor's Office; Plat Book 5, p. 125; Samuel McCoy's *Tippecanoe;* see Boone's *Cave Sepulcher,* by Coulmbia Paxton Wood, in Huntingburg Independent of May 20, 1916; Esarey's *Indiana,* pp. 145, 205 and 246.

[26] The University Society's *Lincoln,* p. 23; Holland's *Lincoln,* p. 25; Herndon & Weik's *Lincoln,* p. 16; Nicolay's *Lincoln,* p. 7.

[27] Plat Book 5, p. 11.

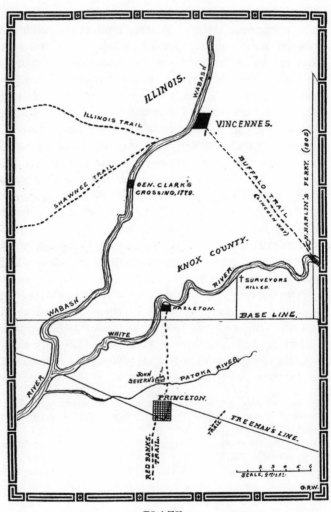

PLATE 2.

Fulda, Mariah Hill, and went north of Dale, almost to the southwest corner of Dubois county, entered Pike county, and seems to have been lost at the Freeman line, two miles northeast of Pleasantville. The "Yellow Banks Trail" came up from Rockport, by way of Chrisney, Gentryville, and joined the "Rome Trace" near the Pike county line. Rome was originally called Washington. It was an early county seat of Perry county. E. Buckingham, William Rector and Levi Barber were early settlers in Perry county. These names are found upon the early surveys of Indiana.[28]

Surveyor Thomas Freeman found a large buffalo trace in Crawford county. It entered Dubois county near Birdseye, near which town is a buffalo wallow. He also made a record of an Indian trail four miles east of Princeton, Indiana, in 1802. This is probably the old trail used by pioneers in traveling from New Harmony, via Princeton, and reaching the Buffalo trace, so as to remain over night at Fort McDonald, at the *Mudholes*. Later government surveyors do not seem to mention this trail from this line to the Ohio. Thomas Freeman, the surveyor mentioned above, also surveyed the north line of Florida, in 1796.

Colonel Josiah Harmer, at the head of a detachment of United States infantry, after marching across the country from a point on the Ohio, at the mouth of Pigeon creek, reached Vincennes on the 19th of July, 1787. He must have gone over the Red Banks Trail.[29]

11

[28] Surveyor's Records of Ranges 1 to 7 inclusive, of land acquired by the treaty of Vincennes, 1804, State Auditor's Office; Miscellaneous Record 1, Indiana, pp. 18 and 19; Esarey's *Indiana,* p. 208; *Indiana, The Public Domain and Its Survey,* map, p. 9. (Note: "Yellow Banks" was in Kentucky, opposite range 6 west, in Indiana.)

[29] Dillon's *Indiana,* pp. 379 and 406; Miscellaneous Record I, Indiana, p. 17; Hume's *Journal of a Visit to the Western Country,* also *Early Travels in Indiana,* p. 520; Brown's *"Western Gazetteer,"* p. 68.

One of the most conspicuous Indian traces in southern Indiana was known as the 'Red Banks Trail," running from what is now Henderson, Kentucky, north by way of Evansville and Princeton to Vincennes. It ran almost due north and south, and practically with what are now the Evansville & Terre Haute Railroad and the Traction Line from Evansville to Princeton. It ran about one mile west of the range line between ranges 10 and 11.[30]

About six miles northwest of Mt. Carmel, Illinois, are located two "beauty spots," so called by Thomas Freeman, the Vincennes tract surveyor, of 1802. Two Indian traces from the south—called roads by the surveyors, joined near there, and probably helped to form the famous "Shawnee trace" that led from southern Illinois to Vincennes. The southwest corner of the Vincennes tract is in section 34, town 1 north, range 14 west, near Fox river, in Illinois. The base line runs east and west about one-half mile south of this corner, and crosses the Freeman line near a half-section corner of section 35. The "Beauty spots" and the two roads are between this Freeman corner and the Wabash river.

General Clark followed an old Indian trace through southern Illinois, and intended to meet his galley and forty men near the mouth of White river before he took Vincennes, February 24, 1779. To do so he would have to follow or cross some or all of these Indian trails, in Illinois, near what afterward became the southwest corner of the Vincennes tract—an Indian gift to the French—unless he followed the "Illinois

12

[30] Plat Book 5. pp. 74, 75 and 76; Indiana Historical Society's Publication 2, p. 464, Vol. 6, p. 296-297 (map) ; Cockrum's *Pioneer History of Indiana,* p. 323.

trace" hereinafter mentioned.[31] The "Hunters' Road" mentioned by General Clark may have joined these traces.[32]

The so-called Illinois trace led west from Vincennes, and
was really the "Old Buffalo trace," from Clark's Grant.[33] The
west line of the Vincennes tract crossed the Illinois trace. The
crossing was almost equidistant from the two corners, on a
prairie, and near a creek. If General Clark came east on this
trace, in 1779, he left it at the Embarrass river, went down the
river, and then over to and across the Wabash. His boat was
to come up the Wabash and meet him at the mouth of White
river, or near it.[34]

An Indian trail led north from Vincennes, and crossed the
Freeman line near Carlisle, about one and one-half miles east
of the northwest corner of the Carlisle offset. It continued
north, passed near Terre Haute, and to Fort Harrison. The
survey records show an excellent map of Fort Harrison and
its ancient environs of 1375.23 acres, known as the "United
States Military Reserve." The reserve began about one mile

13

[31] Plat Book 2, pp. 121 and 124; Plat Book 5, pp. 87 and 177; Mis-
cellaneous Record 1, Indiana, p. 13, State Auditor's Office; Cockrum's
Pioneer History of Indiana, pp. 18, 38, 71 and 150;*The Book of the
Sons of the Revolution in Indiana,* by Wm. Allen Wood, p. 57; Dillon's
Historical Notes of the Northwestern Territory, pp. 153 and 156.

[32] Dillon's *Indiana*, p. 124.

[33] Miscellaneous Record 1, Indiana, p. 10; Plat Book 2, p. 122.

[34] State Geologist's Report, 1873 (map); *Early Travels in Indiana,*
p. 38; *The Western Gazetteer* (1817), p. 39—"principal rapids"; Miscellaneous Record 1, Indiana, p. 10; *Executive Journal, Indiana Territory,* p. 113 (Ferry); same, p. 132; Esarey's *Indiana*, p. 57, map of
Clark's Expedition; Dillon's *Indiana,* p. 141; Ellis' *Life of Daniel
Boone*, p. 94; *The Book of the Sons of the Revolution in Indiana,* p.
57; Dillon's *Historical Notes of the Northwestern Territory,* pp. 156
and 157.

north of Terre Haute, and extended north two miles or more.[35]

In the neighborhood of Odon there were several Indian trails that probably led from Vincennes, or the Delaware town on White river, toward Gosport.[36] Thomas Freeman made a record of Indian trails or roads in the neighborhood of Indian and Trinity Springs, in Martin county.[37]

An Indian trace going from Fort Wayne to Fort Harrison passed near Thorntown, in 1822.[38]

It is apparent from these officially recorded Indian traces or trails that all led toward Vincennes, or its environs. They establish Vincennes as the "Indian capital" of southern Indiana. In places some of these Indian traces have become surface roads, improved highways, "Dixie Highways," and even railroads and traction lines. Many early pioneer roads were blazed from them, but this article is confined to the period when Indians, as well as white men, used them. It is a source of most exquisite pleasure to a surveyor to read the field notes of a government deputy surveyor who was copious in his notations on his official records. Probably they are valued more

14

[35] *Early Travels in Indiana*, p. 68; Brown's *"Western Gazetteer,"* p. 68 and p. 77; Samuel McCoy's novel, *"Tippecanoe,"* pp. 176-179. Thomas Freeman surveyed the Spanish line in Florida, Dillon's *Historical Notes of the Northwestern Territory*, p. 409; Plat Book 2, p. 84, State Auditor's Office; Cockrum's *Pioneer History of Indiana*, pp. 242 and 256; Montgomery's *Life of Harrison*, p. 92; *History of Pike and Dubois Counties*, pp. 96 and 97; Cockrum's *Pioneer History of Indiana*, pp. 358, 361 and 365; Miscellaneous Record 1, Indiana, p. 34; Article 5, Treaty of Ft. Wayne, 1803; Senate Documents, Vol. 39, pp. 64 and 65; Esarey's *Indiana*, pp. 38 and 110; Beard's *"The Battle of Tippecanoe,"* page 52; Dillon's *Indiana*, pp. 157, 158 and 447. Read *"On the Wea Trail,"* a novel by Caroline Brown, p. 106. McCoy's *"Tippecanoe,"* pp. 176 and 179.

[36] See Freeman survey; Cockrum's *Pioneer History of Indiana*, p. 351.

[37] Miscellaneous Record 1, Indiana, pp. 26 and 27; Plat Book 2, p. 55.

[38] Miscellaneous Record 1, Indiana, p. 265.

now than when he made them. An observant deputy might
record a small Indian path or road, while one not so observant
might easily fail to record a more prominent trace. However, the survey records refer to the old trails with such fre-
quency that where no mention is made of them their location
may be determined with a fair degree of accuracy by tradition,

PLATE 3.

The broken lines in the map above represent the old trails as
indicated on the maps of the government surveyors. Local tradition,
the topography, roads long in use, military orders and letters or de-
scriptions written by early travelers all prove the records, and by a
general knowledge these known points may be united and a fairly good
map of the early roads would result.

topography, or circumstantial evidence. A careful pioneer draughtsman saw that his map indicated the trails, while an indifferent one produced a fairly good plat with the trails omitted as of no permanent value or interest. All this must be taken into consideration when forming a conclusion. The surveyors' ranges are six miles wide, and while one surveyor may have omitted recording a trail through his range, the other ones, joining him made a record of it, thus the general trend is found, beyond the shadow of a doubt. Traces were recorded on the maps as guides to men who desired to buy land without seeing it, and for military purposes.[39]

On some of these trails "houses of entertainment" were erected by private or public enterprise.[40]

THE BUFFALO TRACE.

16

In pioneer days the line of least resistance was the line of travel, hence streams were the lines of travel, when possible.[41] When streams did not lead to the desired destination, forest paths were used. In time these became bridle paths, sled roads, wagon roads, etc. Thus animal paths, Indian trails, military roads, etc., became highways. When it was possible these old paths were on ridges, and usually watersheds. Settlements were made on these paths, and eventually the line of travel became the line of intelligence. Men and animals did not travel in straight lines, for they preferred a sure footing and a hard path to water and swamps.

The Buffalo trace, "spacious enough for two wagons to go

39 Brown's *Western Gazetteer* (1817), p. 44, p. 62; Barnes' *United States History,* p. 159.

40 Petitions to Congress, 1800-1802. Indiana Historical Society's Publication 2, pp. 455-470; American State Papers, *Indian Affairs,* Vol. 1. p. 688.

41 Smith's *"Early Indiana Trials and Sketches,"* p. 116.

abreast," was the one big overland highway in southern Indiana. It was so prominent that it was used as a basis from which to locate a treaty line between General William Henry Harrison and the Indians, in 1804. The treaty in question referred to the trace as the boundary line, but since it was a line of travel it made an inconvenient treaty line. The treaty reads: "And as it is the intention of the parties to these presents that the whole of the said road shall be within the tract ceded to the United States, it is agreed that the boundary in that quarter shall be a straight line, to be drawn parallel to the course of the said road, from the eastern boundary of the tract ceded by the treaty of Fort Wayne, to Clark's Grant, but the said line is not to pass at a greater distance than half a mile from the most northerly bend in said road."[42]

In order to locate this straight line, as called for by the treaty, it was necessary to first survey the old trace by chain and compass, which was done, and these "calls" having been made a matter of official record, enable us to locate definitely the old trace for a distance of nearly forty-four miles.[43] The survey of the old "Vincennes trail," or "Buffalo trace" was begun July 11, 1805, by Surveyor William Rector. It began at the "Parker Improvements" on the west line of Clark's Grant, and about one and one-half miles from the Ohio river. It crossed the east fork of Buck creek about three and one-half miles from "Parker's Improvement." Nine miles from Clark's Grant there was a "cabin near the spring."

The trace crossed Indian creek. At each mile along the trace Surveyor Rector marked trees thus: "To C. G. 26 mi.," etc., as the distance might be. It meant "To Clarks Grant, — miles." On July 15, 1895, he camped at Sullivan's Spring,

17

[42] American State Papers, Class 2, *Indian Affairs*, pp. 689 and 690; Senate Documents, Vol. 39, pp. 70, 71 and 72.

[43] *Centennial History and Handbook of Indiana*, p. 31; Smith's *Indiana*, Vol. I, pp. 163, 165, 230, 232, 235-239; Dillon's *Indiana*, p. 419.

18

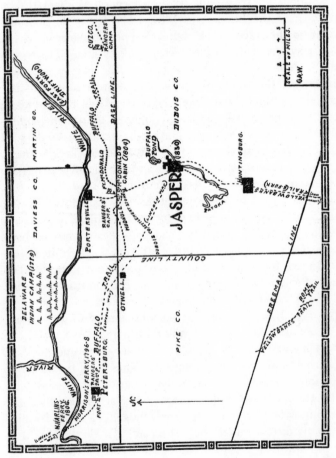

PLATE 4.

about thirty-one and one-eighth miles from Clark's Grant. The record shows that Samuel Hay lived on the west bank of Little Blue river, about thirty-four and one-fourth miles from Clark's Grant, and where the trace crossed the river. There was a "whet stone cave" on the trace forty-three miles and seven chains from Clark's Grant. This was near where the trace entered the Vincennes tract, and not far from French Lick Springs.[44]

Through the Vincennes tract, covering a distance of about sixty miles, the location of the trace may be officially determined, at sixty points, or more. The surveyors who subdivided the tract into sections made a record showing how far the trace was from a nearby section corner, thus the entire trace through Indiana may be determined.

After entering the Vincennes tract south of Paoli, the trace practically follows Buckingham's base line through Columbia, Harbison and Boone townships, in Dubois county, and west in Pike county, until it reaches Petersburg, Indiana, then it goes northwest to Vincennes, crossing White river at "N. Harlin's ferry," at the range line, six miles west of the fork of White river.[45]

In Dubois county the animals wallowed in the mud at the

[44] State Geologist's Report (Cox) 1875, pp. 226-230; Miscellaneous Record 1, Indiana, pp. 37-46, State Auditor's Office; Esarey's *History of Indiana*, p. 145; Indiana Historical Society's Publication, Vol. 4. pp. 190 and 262; Vol. 3. p. 97.

[45] Plat Book 5, p. 27; Indianapolis News, 1915; Cockrum's *Pioneer History of Indiana*, pp. 208, 490 and 525; Record 9, pp. 403, 411 and 425 N. & W., State Auditor's Office; Dillon's *Indiana*, pp. 403 and 419; History of Pike and Dubois Counties, pp. 475 and 476; Indiana Historical Society's Publication, Vol. 4, pp. 383-389; "The Public Domain and its Surveys," p. 9; Wilson's *History of Dubois County*, pp. 27, 31 and 163; Esarey's *Indiana*, pp. 341-345; The Western Gazetteer, 1817, p. 40.

famous "Mudhole," and found water and cane at the Buffalo pond two miles northeast of Jasper. The surveyor's map which locates and names this pond also locates the Mudholes and Mc-Donald's cabin. Some of the buffalo wallows were upon the farm now owned by John Mehne, of Dubois county. To this

20

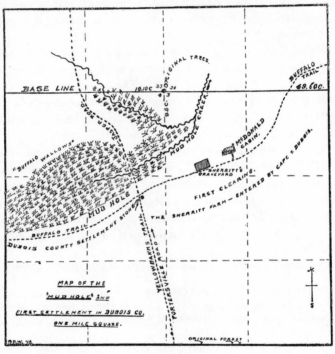

PLATE 5.

day buffalo bones are occasionally found in the marshes on this farm.

Fort MacDonald, at the Mudholes, was a stopping place for travelers, one night out of Princeton. In an early volume known as "Hulme's Journal of a Visit to the Western Countries," in speaking of traveling out of Princeton, Indiana, he says: "We spent the first night at a place very appropriately called Mudholes, a sort of fort for guarding against Indians."

The Buffalo traces were of no mean consideration in early Indiana life. The buffalo was a large, heavy animal with a comparatively small foot. He could not cross low, swampy, marshy land, and being gregarious, he could not remain long in one place, for hundreds and sometimes thousands of them ranged together. Their pastures vanished rapidly, and they had to move frequently. Buffalo roads, therefore, were very definitely marked and well beaten. The Miami Indian name for a "buffalo road" was "Lan-an-zo-ki-mi-wi.

The small feet of these animals, along with their heavy bodies, necessitated their roads following the highlands—indeed the ridges, or watersheds.[46] The Indians followed these trails because they were open, and occasionally furnished game. When the white man came as an explorer, hunter or settler, he followed these lines of least resistance. The buffalo avoided the hill and the swamp, and therefore took the ridge or the valley. He was a good civil engineer and path-finder. In fact he found the road and man followed in his footsteps.[47]

But a little more than a hundred years ago, vast herds of buffaloes grazed over the plains and prairies of Indiana during the summer season. They were few in the timber-lands, but numberless on the plains and prairies. In spring they came north from Kentucky into Indiana and covered the plains in

21

[46] Venable's *"Footprints of the Pioneers,"* pp. 69 and 70; History of Pike and Dubois Counties, pp. 245 and 246.

[47] Wilson's *History of Dubois County,* pp. 25, 31, 101 and 346; Indiana Historical Society's Publication, Vol. 4, pp. 383 and 384, Vol. 6, pp. 291-296 (map); for a good description of the buffalo, read pp. 427 and 428, Cockrum's *Pioneer History of Indiana.*

great armies, then, as winter approached, retreated to the borders of the large rivers where they sheltered in the forest and fed upon the boundless fields of wild cane.[48]

As the buffaloes moved back and forth in spring and fall, they so beat down the earth that their traces still remain, particularly in Floyd and Orange counties. The tall grass of the prairies was divided by paths made by the buffaloes as they grazed in long, unbroken lines. These small trails that checked the prairies all led into one great trail made in their journeyings to and from the pasture lands. Colonel Croghan, an efficient officer, wrote that the country was full of buffaloes.

That the buffalo was a common ranger in southern Indiana is recalled by the fact that Colonel Archibald Loughery's men, in 1790, were dressing a buffalo, near the corner of Ohio and Dearborn counties, on the banks of the Ohio river, when they were ambushed by Indians, at what is now known as Loughery's creek. In the battle that ensued, in the river, nearly all the Americans (107) were killed or taken prisoners. This disaster was so severely felt that General Clark was compelled to abandon his contemplated attack on Detroit. A very little thing, on more than one occasion, has changed the boundaries of a nation.[49]

The favorite winter resorts of the buffaloes that fed on the pasturage of Indiana were the Big Bone and Blue Licks of Kentucky. To these salt springs they came in armies too great to be numbered. The earth for miles around their meeting places was beaten bare by the hoofs of these restless hordes. Evidence of their former abundance (1784) is pre-

48 Esarey's *Indiana*, p. 38.

49 Esarey's *Indiana*, p. 85; Dillon's *Historical Notes of the Northwestern Territory*, p. 192; Dillon's *Indiana*, p. 173; Cockrum's *Pioneer History of Indiana*, pp. 61 and 126; Indiana Historical Society's Publication, Vol. 1, p. 133, Vol. 2, pp. 107, 112, 126 and 159.

served in the swamps about the Big Bone Lick. In places their bones are massed to the depth of two feet or more, as close as the stones of a pavement, and so beaten down by succeeding herds as to make it difficult to lift them from their beds.

It is said that in their migrations they obstructed the Ohio river for miles. On his voyage down the Ohio, Colonel Croghan frequently wrote in his journal of the great herds of buffaloes seen by him.[50] It was told by the Indians that all the buffaloes of this region perished near the beginning of the last century. One winter the country was swept by a "great cold." The snow lay deep on the ground for many months, and the animals could find no food. The cold and snow continued until they all died, and long afterward their bones lay bleaching on the plains where they fell alone or in herds.

The buffalo, it seems, was worshipped by the Prairie Indians, and that gave missionary Mermet, at Vincennes, in or about 1702, an opportunity to lead the Indians from the Manitou, or Spirit of the buffalo, which was under the earth and animated all buffaloes, etc., to the idea that *men* ought to have a Manitou who inhabits them, etc. The missionary tried to lead the Indians, in this way, from the known to the unknown, in the way of religion. Whether he succeeded or not, the report proves that the buffalo had the sincere consideration of the Indian. The buffalo is remembered on the flag of Wyoming, on the flag of the Secretary of the Interior, and upon the five cent piece.[51]

23

[50] Cockrum's *Pioneer History of Indiana*, p. 18; Smith's *Indiana*, p. 163; Smith's *"Early Indiana Trials and Sketches"* under Daniel Boone, p. 468; Gen. Simon Kenton, in *Life of Daniel Boone*, by Edw. S. Ellis, pp. 217 and 218; *Daniel Boone and The Wilderness Road*, by Bruce, p. 110; *Stories of Columbia*, by Glascock, pp. 36, 51 and 138 to 148; Dillon's *History of Indiana*, pp. 84 and 401.

[51] *The National Geographical Magazine*, October, 1917, pp. 334 and 335; *Early Travels in Indiana*, pp. 116, 322, 520 and 521; Dillon's *Indiana*, p. 22.

In some parts of Indiana the Indian trail and buffalo trace are the same. They were paths beaten by both, and for both they were public highways across the plains, or through the forest.[52]

The trails and traces were great highways over which civilization came into the wilderness. Wild animals often followed the trails, trappers followed the game, and settlers followed the trappers. The backwoodsmen of the east came west, forded rivers, chose their resting place, and erected a palisade fort to protect their rude homes. Thus the west developed.[53] Each important trail was as well known to the Indians and emigrants as are the chief roads known to us. It was important that each new-comer should know the trail by which he came and the place to which it led. Outside of these there was little other than a trackless wood, and for many years after the first settlements were formed these remained the gateways to the west. For many years the pack horses came over the trail along the Ohio from its fall to Vincennes on the Wabash. Both the French and the English pushed into the interior over the trail from Vincennes to Lafayette.

In 1788, General Harmar and his army traveled over this Buffalo trace, traveling the 130 miles in six days. He observed that the country was hilly, but excellent for wheat, an observation now known to be true.[54]

Along these trails the emigrants traveled in search of land on which to settle, and fur traders carried their furs to market. Along these pack horses threaded their way, loaded with simple articles precious to the pioneers. Along these there came

[52] History of Pike and Dubois Counties, p. 271.

[53] Burton's *United States History,* pp. 176 and 177. Read *"On The We-a Trail,"* a novel by Caroline Brown.

[54] Esarey's *Indiana,* p. 98.

the power that conquered the wilderness and compelled it to yield up its hidden wealth to enrich humanity.[55]

Many people from Virginia, Maryland and the farther east took passage on steamboats at Pittsburg and stopped at the Falls. The Buffalo trace led west from there, and soon became a prominent line of travel. It became a practical outlet to the west.

The old trace that crossed the Ohio river at Louisville, Kentucky, known to the white people as the Clarksville and Vincennes trace, that had been a main traveled way from time immemorial, was the most favored route, and two-thirds of all the early settlers who came to southern Indiana, west of Louisville, came over that route. On a second visit to Vincennes, in 1786, after his famous capture of that post, General Clark marched about 1,000 men over the Buffalo trace, from the Falls of the Ohio to Vincennes. This was in 1786, and after he had conquered the great Northwest and given an empire to his country.[56]

The first post office in Pike county (Petersburg, Indiana) was in charge of Hosea Smith at White Oak Springs, in 1811. Smith was postmaster, surveyor, justice of the peace, mer-

25

[55] *History of Indiana*, by Goodrich and Tuttle, pp. 17, 18 and 45; Glascock's *Young Folks' Indiana*, pp. 159-161; "The Pioneer Women," in Pike County Democrat, March 10, 1916, written by Mrs. S. W. Chappell; Dillon's *Indiana*, p. 187; Secret Journals of Congress, Vol. 4, p. 311; Esarey's *Indiana*, pp. 95, 98 and 245; Cockrum's *Pioneer History of Indiana*, pp. 18 and and 19; Venable's "Footprints of the Pioneers," pp. 70 and 71.

[56] *Early Travels in Indiana*, pp. 232, 291; Brown's "Western Gazetteer" (1817), pp. 62, 63 and 77; Dillon's *Historical Notes of the Northwestern Territory*, pp. 170, 202 and 203; Dillon's *Indiana*, p. 185; Esarey's *Indiana*, p. 95; Cockrum's *Pioneer History of Indiana*, pp. 18, 61, 63, 157, 215 and 556; Wilson's *History of Dubois County*, pp. 27, 31, 100, 158 and 163.

chant and farmer. The office was on an old Indian trace leading from Vincennes to Louisville. The road led from White
river, at Decker's Ferry, White Oak Springs, Mudholes, near
Ireland, Dubois county, (south of) French Lick, Paoli, to
Louisville. George Teverbaugh carried the mail over this route
once a week on foot; however, Mathias Mounts was the first
carrier. When Indiana became a territory "the mode of com-
munication between the Ohio Falls, Vincennes and the farther
western stations was along this old Indian trace connecting
these places, which had been there from time immemorial."[57]

The stage coach followed on the trail of the pioneers.
Early in the spring of 1820 a Mr. Foyles started a stage line
from Louisville to Vincennes. The advertisement stated that
it was the first line to be established in the state. This is perhaps true. The trace from Louisville to Vincennes is the
oldest in the state. At first it ran along the boundary between
Crawford and Orange counties following the south bank of
Driftwood and crossing White river north of Petersburg
But the settlement of the towns of Washington, Mt. Pleasant,
Hindostan and Paoli caused most travelers to go by the northern route. It was over these routes that Foyles established his
stage line, using whichever road seemed best.[58] The east

26

[57] Goodspeed Brothers' *History of Pike and Dubois Counties*, 1885,
p. 251; Cockrum's *Pioneer History of Indiana*, pp. 132 and 169; Indiana Historical Society's Publications, Vol. 2, p. 366, Vol. 6, see map,
p. 296; (see Vol. 3, p. 116, for Decker's Ferry license).

[58] Esarey's *History of Indiana*, 1915, pp. 246 and 261; Wilson's *History of Dubois County*, p. 27; Cockrum's *Pioneer History of Indiana*,
p. 348. McCoy's *"Tippecanoe,"* p. 130. Mail was carried from Vincennes to Louisville. See *"Tippecanoe,"* p. 145. Indiana Historical
Society's Publications, Vol. 5, pp. 56 and 112; *Early Travels in Indiana*,
pp. 138 and 142, 236 and 237, 256 and 257, 274, 279 and 294; The Western Gazetteer (1817), pp. 38, 40-44.

fork of White river used to be called "Driftwood," also the "Muddy fork."

The old Buffalo trace was patrolled by rangers to protect the emigrants. The rangers of 1807 were foot soldiers; those of 1812 were mounted. On April 20, 1807, these orders were issued at Vincennes: "You are to patrol the old Indian trace that leads from this place to Clarksville, on the Ohio river, from a point where this old road crosses White river and going as far as thirty-five miles east of the Mudholes."[59]

The Mudholes was on the Portersville and Jasper road, and thirty-five miles east would reach the rangers' camp where the Blue river trace intersects this trace, or where the rangers of General John Tipton began.[60] The Buffalo trace crossed White river at N. Harlan's ferry, six miles west of where the river forks. That would make the patrol cover fifty-five miles. The trace received unusual attention in the way of military patrols, and a good guard was kept at White Oak Springs (Petersburg) on the trace for a long time.[61] Horse stealing by the Indians had to be guarded against very carefully. Sergeant Hogue was a scout on the trace.

The paper upon which was printed an early territorial code of Indiana (1807) was carried over the Buffalo trace from Georgetown, Kentucky.[62]

The rangers on the old Buffalo trace had a camp at Mil-

27

[59] *Readings in Indiana History,* p. 99.

[60] General John Tipton, in Smith's *"Early Indiana Trials and Sketches,"* p. 478; Cockrum's *Pioneer History of Indiana,* pp. 202, 203, 228 and 371.

[61] Cockrum's *Pioneer History of Indiana,* pp. 200, 204, 206, 208, 371 and 372; same, 210, 228 and 229; Montgomery's *Life of Harrison,* p. 70; *History of Pike and Dubois Counties,* p. 369.

[62] Dillon's *History of Indiana,* p. 421; History of Pike and Dubois Counties, p. 84; Indiana Historical Society's Publications, Vol. 2, pp. 17 and 143.

burn's Springs, at Cuzco, in Dubois county. Dubois county was settled at the Mudholes, by the McDonald family, and its first courts were held at the McDonald cabin. The cabin had been erected before 1804, for its location is indicated upon the survey maps of 1804.[63]

In 1807 or 1808, the Gurney family, of Jefferson county, Kentucky, came into Dubois and Pike counties over the old Buffalo trace, going as far west as White Oak Springs, now known as Petersburg. Woolsey Pride had built a fort there. The rangers protected the family on its trip to the fort, and the family was instructed by General Harrison to remain at the fort until the Indians had quieted down. Gurney disobeyed orders, and started back saying he was going to the Mudholes. He and his family did not go to the Mudholes, but went near Velpen, and in time the father and son were killed by panthers. One day John and William McDonald, who had a home at the Mudholes, found Mrs. Gurney and her little daughter who were trying to find the "Kentucky road." (This is the Buffalo trace.) The McDonalds took care of the wanderers, and in time got them back into Kentucky.[64]

These McDonalds had many fights with the Indians, and in one case with several Indians who had taken two white women and two children as prisoners, in Kentucky. Following the Yellow Banks trail to the Buffalo trace, they stole McDonald's horse, and went on east, or southeast. Probably they had started for an Indian cave west of the town of Dubois.[65] The Indians were overtaken by the McDonalds, Enlows, and

[63] Wilson's *History of Dubois County*, pp. 352 and 353; Plat Book 5, p. 27, State Auditor's Office. Samuel McCoy's novel, *"Tippecanoe,"* p. 129.

[64] Cockrum's *Pioneer History of Indiana*, pp. 207, 208, 221 and 222; 486 and 487; Wilson's *History of Dubois County*, p. 27; Dillon's *Indiana*, p. 439.

[65] Wilson's *History of Dubois County*, pp. 69 and 87.

others. Eight Indians were killed, and their captives liberated. This Indian battle took place on Patoka river west of the town of Dubois.[66]

In 1807, a pioneer by the name of Larkins was killed by the Indians, near where the Buffalo trace crosses the county line between Dubois and Pike counties. His wife and five children were taken into captivity.

Many narrow escapes are recorded as having taken place along these Indian trails. Even the government surveyors had to be on their guard. Panthers were constantly to be guarded against. They seem to have been in the habit of crouching upon the limbs overhanging the trails. These wild animals were as dangerous as the Indians.[67]

Occasionally the Indians had a reason to be vicious. Many of the settlers, like the uncle of Abraham Lincoln, thought it a virtuous act to shoot an Indian at sighht. In fact the murder of Indians was not considered murder at all.[68]

In 1807, Captain Hargrove's rangers captured a British spy on the Buffalo trace, and sent him to the fort at Vincennes. The spy may have been holding conferences with the Indians, for the battle of Tippecanoe, and the War of 1812 were "in the making."[69]

29

[66] Cockrum's *Pioneer History of Indiana,* pp. 180, 201, 203, 206, 234, 496 and 499.

[67] Cockrum's *Pioneer History of Indiana,* pp. 111, 119, 156, 208, 221, 371, 441, 464, 482, 485, 488 and 489; *History of Pike and Dubois Counties,* pp. 47 and 261; *History of Indiana,* by Goodrich and Tuttle, p. 54 For a description of the panther's acts, see pp. 156-157 *"Tippecanoe."*

[68] Henry Adams' *United States History,* Volume 6, p. 72; Indiana Historical Society's Publication, Vol. 4, p. 232; History of Pike and Dubois Counties, p. 482; Cockrum's *Pioneer History of Indiana,* pp. 173, 204 and 205; Dillon's *Indiana,* note on page 112, note page 424.

[69] Cockrum's *Pioneer History of Indiana,* pp. 219, 220 and 224; History of Pike and Dubois Counties, p. 336. Read *"On The We-a Trail,"* a novel, by Caroline Brown.

With all this wild animal and Indian danger hundreds of
families, Indians, colored slaves and prominent pioneer states-
men traveled over this old route. In 1799, Judge Jacob Burnet,
Arthur St. Clair, Jr., and a Mr. Morrison traveled over this
road and had a thrilling experience. They met Indians, buffaloes, wild cats, panthers, etc., but arrived at Vincennes in
four days after leaving the Falls of the Ohio. They were on
horseback. A tavern keeper on the New Albany and Vincennes road stated that upwards of 5,000 souls had passed his
tavern on their way to Missouri during the year 1819.

A pioneer whose name was Morrison conducted a ferry
across White river at Tanner's Station, at or near Petersburg
between 1796-1798. Later he moved to Aurora, Indiana.[70]

A study of the "Knobs" near New Albany, and a knowledge
of the old Buffalo trace enables one to understand the seal of
Indiana.[71]

In 1915, the legislature of Indiana authorized the Governor
to appoint a commission to determine the route traveled by
Abraham Lincoln and his father's family when they moved
from Indiana to Illinois, in 1830. Governor Ralston appointed
Hon. Joseph M. Cravens, of Madison, and Hon. Jesse W.
Weik, of Greencastle, as the commission. On December 15,
1916, the commission reported that "they [the Lincolns]
moved northward through Dale to Jasper, thence northwest-
wardly through the villages of Ireland, Otwell and Algiers to
Petersburg, at or near which place they crossed White river

[70] Indiana Historical Society's Publications, Vol. 2, p. 366; Esarey's
Indiana, pp. 143, 145, 180 and 245; Burnett's Notes, pp. 72-75; Indiana
Historical Society's Publication, Vol. 4, p. 190, Vol. 2, p. 366.

[71] Centennial History and Handbook of Indiana, p. 71; Cockrum's
Pioneer History of Indiana, pp. 132, 134, 141 and 163; Wilson's *History of Dubois County*, p. 35; Brown's *"Western Gazetteer"* (1817),
p. 44.

and then pushed on to Vincennes, by the most direct route." The road from Lincoln City to Jasper was a branch of the "Yellow Banks trail," the road from Jasper to near Otwell was a branch of the Buffalo trail, and the road from near Otwell to Vincennes was the Buffalo trail. The county commissioners' courts of the various counties have named the above route the "LINCOLN WAY."[72]

Many pioneer forts were built along the old Buffalo trace, or near it. There was a fort at Petersburg. Ft. McDonald, at the Mudholes, and Ft. Butler and Ft. Farris, near by, were in Dubois county. There was a rangers' camp at Cuzco, in Dubois county, equi-distant between Vincennes and Louisville, and one at Blue river where the old trace crossed the river.[73] Northwest of Cuzco General Harrison improved the old trace. Logs used in the improvement yet remain under the road bed. Old graves are near the camp at Cuzco.

31

On October 9, 1834, this appeared in the Paoli Patriot: "We presume not less than one hundred and fifty wagons have passed through this village in the last two weeks." That indicates the line of travel and the amount of travel.[74]

In Dubois county, where the Yellow Banks trail crosses the Buffalo trail, a marker is being placed. It is of Bedford

[72] Report of the Lincoln Highway Commission, 1916, pp. 4 and 17; "The Lincoln Way," Ililnois State Historical Library, Reports of 1913 and 1915; Indiana Historical Society's Publications, Vol. 2, p. 366; See "N. Harlan's Ferry," hereinafter; Governor's Message to the General Assembly of 1917. Records of Commissioners' Courts, 1917.

[73] Esarey's *Indiana*, pp. 190, 198, 205 and 207; Wilson's *History of Dubois County*, pp. 29, 27, 74, 108, 162, 284; Indiana Historical Society's Publication, Vol. 2, pp. 131 and 197; History of Pike and Dubois Counties, pp. 478 and 482.

[74] Esarey's *Indiana*, p. 276; *Early Travels in Indiana*, pp. 194 and 209; Brown's *"Western Gazetteer,"* pp. 64 and 65.

stone, weighs 8,000 pounds, and is nearly nine feet high. The inscription reads as follows:

1801.

DUBOIS COUNTY SETTLEMENT STONE.

"The Mudholes on the Buffalo Trail."

This is the Oldest White Settlement in Dubois County. Here the McDonald Family Settled in 1801.

Erected by

GEO. R. WILSON, C. E.

1919.

VALLONIA TRACE.

32   On the Indian trace between Vallonia, the primitive and temporary county seat of Jackson county, and the old town of Springville, in Clark county, stands a log cabin known as the "Aaron Burr cabin." It is about one and one-half miles southeast from where the old fort stood at Vallonia.[75] Tradition records Aaron Burr as having stayed there one night during his famous conspiracy days of 1806. The occupant may have been some poor misguided follower of Colonel Burr.[76] The cabin is fairly well preserved. In 1807, the people about the Ohio Falls were much agitated over the unpatriotic movements of Aaron Burr. Boats had been built at the Falls under his direction, and a large drove of horses were at hand.[77] General Harrison instructed his militia commanders to assist these misguided followers of Burr to find homes in the wilderness, and give them military protection on the

---

[75] Clarence L. W. Turmail, Vallonia, Indiana.

[76] Cockrum's *Pioneer History of Indiana,* pp. 213, 219, 471 and 472.

[77] *History of Indiana,* by Goodrich and Tuttle, p. 141; Barnes' *United States History,* note on page 157.

theory that they would "make as good citizens as any."[78]
There were many Burr followers in the northern part of Perry,
Spencer and Warrick counties.

Not far from Vallonia, General John Tipton fought a fierce
battle with the Indians.[79]

After the Pigeon Roost Massacre, in Scott county, in September, 1812, a large force of the Clark county militia gath-
ered from the vicinity of Charlestown to pursue the Indians.
The militia pursued the savages along this old trail until where
it crossed the Muskackituck. This river was so much swollen
that the militia could not effect a crossing, and it was compelled to give up the pursuit. This massacre and the Indian
attack on Fort Harrison were synchronical, both September
3, 1812.[80]

Vallonia has an Indian history interesting in itself, not to
mention its prominence in pioneer days along other lines.[81]

33

BLUE RIVER TRACE.

There was an Indian trace near the mouth of Blue river, at
Fredonia. Many of the emigrants that came over this trace

[78] Cockrum's *Pioneer History of Indiana,* pp. 213, 214, 373 and 471;
Indiana Historical Society's Publication, Vol. 3, note foot of p. 177;
also Vol. 2, pp. 24 and 75; Esarey's *Indiana,* pp. 177, 178 and 246;
"An Historic Cabin," in Jackson County Democrat, 1852; Dillon's *Indiana,* pp. 431 and 432; Esarey's *Indiana,* pp. 177 and 246.

[79] Battle of Tipton's Island, Indianapolis News, July, 1913; Esarey's
Indiana, pp. 199 and 200.

[80] Indiana Historical Society's Publication, Vol. 2, pp. 128-134; Cock-
rum's *Pioneer History of Indiana,* pp. 354, 355, 360 and 440; Dillon's
Indiana, pp. 491-494; Esarey's *Indiana,* p. 193; Indiana and Indianans,
Vol. 1, p. 93.

[81] Dillon's *Indiana,* pp. 521-525; *Early Travels in Indiana,* p. 49.

34

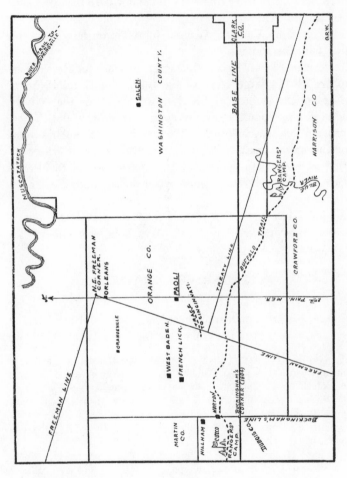

PLATE 6.

found a forest home in Harrison and Washington counties.[82] This trace led from the Ohio river to the Buffalo trace, probably near Hardinsburg and on north. A short distance west of Blue river, on the Buffalo trace, there was a rangers' camp. Here the Buffalo trace rangers had a division. The eastern division was in charge of John Tipton, afterward a United States senator. The men on the western division were commanded by Captain William Hargrove, a pioneer settler of Gibson county. He was born in South Carolina, in 1775, and served as an Indian scout in Kentucky. He saw service at Tippecanoe, and died in 1843. He lived near Princeton, where his descendants are prominent unto this day. It is quite likely the division was near the junction of the Blue river and the Buffalo trace, once a corner of Clark and Knox counties, (1801).[83]

In General Harrison's order of September 1, 1807, to "William Hargrove, commanding first division of rangers, east of the Wabash river," we read: "There has been a trace cut from the Clarksville and Vincennes road that leaves that route at a point about forty miles east of the Mudholes and running south, coming to the Ohio river at the west end of a large bend three miles west of the mouth of Blue river. There is a traveled way that comes to the south bank of the Ohio opposite this point that runs to the south and far into Kentucky, and people coming to this and other sections of Indiana territory are crossing the river at that point and following Blue river to the old Indian road before mentioned. The two traces to the

35

---

[82] Cockrum's *Pioneer Indiana*, pp. 157, 372 and 485. McCoy's novel, "*Tippecanoe*," p. 145.

[83] Cockrum's *Pioneer History of Indiana*, pp. 203, 223, 349, 350 and 485; Executive Journal, Indiana Territory, p. 2; Indiana Historical Society's Publication, Vol. 3, pp. 97 and 174, General Tipton, born in Tennessee, 1786; Esarey's *Indiana*, pp. 143 to 145.

east which are now being opened should go into this Blue river trace." [84] This trace ran from Fredonia to where the Blue river trace intersected the Buffalo trace, near Samuel Hay's cabin on the west bank of Little Blue river, about thirty-four and one-fourth miles from Clark's Grant.[85] The Mud-holes were two miles south of Portersville, in Dubois county.[86] A road, locally known as the "Fredonia road," led to the west from Fredonia.

In an advertisement which appeared in the Vincennes Sun, June 6, 1818, Fredonia town lots were offered for sale. These words appear in the notice: "A most excellent road can be had and will be opened shortly to Paoli," etc.

In Cockrum's *Pioneer History of Indiana,* pages 482-485, a story is related of Indian and panther fights, typical of many related by the pioneers. This particular story relates to the Buffalo and Blue river traces, etc.

36

YELLOW BANKS TRAIL.

An Indian trail known as the "Yellow Banks trail" started from the Ohio river, at Rockport, and ran north through Spencer, Warrick and Pike counties to the old Delaware Indian summer camp at the forks of White river. This Indian town was the camp of some Delaware Indians that the Piankeshaws had permitted to settle there. The Delawares plundered some traders on the old Buffalo trace, and Captain Helm, under orders from General Clark, destroyed the town. This was in 1779.

There were some far-seeing men in the main body of the

[84] Cockrum's *Pioneer History of Indiana,* p. 215.
[85] Miscellaneous Record, Indiana, pp. 37-46.
[86] Plat Book 5, p. 27, State Auditor's Office; Esarey's *Indiana,* p. 246.

Delaware Indians, of which nation the Delaware Indians in southern Indiana were a part. An early American Congress, at the request of friendly Delaware Indians, promised to send to them "a suitable minister," "a schoolmaster," and "a sober man," to instruct them in the Christian religion, in letters, and in agriculture and other branches of useful knowledge.[87]

A fork of the Yellow Banks trail entered Dubois county just north of Dale, and went north to Portersville, and into Daviess county. Settlements made in Dubois county previous to 1830 indicate its location.[88] The trail from the forks of White river south to Yellow Banks (below Rockport) was patrolled once each week by three soldiers and one scout. It is likely Scout FuQuay served on this route. They were to protect emigrants and report any Indian troubles, etc. Governor Harrison issued such an order to Captain William Hargrove, April 29, 1807.

The Delaware Indians called Yellow Banks "Weesoe Wusapinuk." "Yellow Banks" were so named by reason of the color of the river banks, at Owensboro, Kentucky.[89]

Very likely this trail crossed the Buffalo trace in the environs of Otwell, perhaps near the three mounds north of Otwell, for they would be a natural landmark.[90] In time a military road was cut out from the crossing toward New Albany by way of the Indian ford across Patoka river, at Jasper. This

37

[87] Indian camps along White River, see Brown's *"Western Gazetteer,"* p. 65; Dillon's *Historical Notes of the Northwestern Territory,* pp. 110, 111, 181 and 182; Dillon's *Indiana,* pp. 164 and 165; Esarey's *Indiana,* pp. 79 and 246; Cockrum's *Pioneer History of Indiana,* pp. 58, 59, 127, 156, 167, 172, 477 and 478.

[88] Wilson's *History of Dubois County,* p. 158.

[89] Cockrum's *Pioneer History of Indiana,* pp. 205, 206 and 214; Indiana Historical Society's Publication, Vol. 2, p. 131, Vol. 6, pp. 290 and 296; *Early Travels in Indiana,* p. 27.

[90] History of Pike and Dubois Counties, p. 270.

38

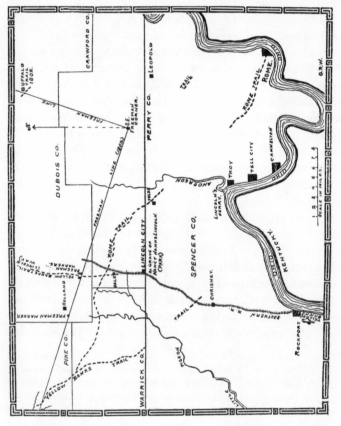

PLATE 7.

may have started from a stockade ordered built, July 11, 1812, or perhaps the stockade was ordered built at the junction of these two routes.[91] The Rome trail united with the Yellow Banks trail near Selvin.[92] In his order to have a military road cut out, General Harrison, on August 20, 1807, wrote Captain Hargrove as follows:

"The trace just south of the Patoka river opened some time ago, will be extended from the Yellow Banks trace, thirty or forty miles east. You had better have the same men go over this route as soon as Severns is through with the new survey farther south. Mr. Severns says that in going near the Patoka river many abrupt banks and deep gorges are met with. Inform him that it is not necessary to make a straight line but to blaze and mark it that it can be easily traced. It is not intended for wheeled vehicles or sleds to pass over but for foot soldiers only. The logs need not be moved but the brush had better be cut seven or eight feet wide."[93]

Thus the old Indian traces running north and south were to be crossed by military roads running east and west, between the Ohio river and the Buffalo trace. These military roads were supplied with a patrol of two men and a scout.[94] John Severns, mentioned hereinbefore, had been living with and near the Indians, was acquainted with them, could talk their dialects, and had been a scout through all lands drained by the White and Patoka rivers.

John FuQuay, a scout, told General Gibson, Secretary for Indiana Territory, in 1802, when asked if it would be safe to survey the land between the Ohio and White rivers, that:

[91] Cockrum's *Pioneer History of Indiana,* pp 215, 216 and 349.

[92] Cockrum's *Pioneer History of Indiana,* pp. 179, 212 and 215;. Esarey's *Indiana,* p. 207.

[93] Cockrum's *Pioneer History of Indiana,* p. 215.

[94] Cockrum's *Pioneer History of Indiana,* pp. 166 and 216.

"There is an old Indian trace running from the Yellow Banks
to the headquarters of the Little Pigeon, where there has been
a large Indian town, then in a northwesterly direction to a
large spring, then along the spring branch to little Patoka, and
it crosses the large Patoka at a good ford and continues to the
forks of White river."[95] It is thought the spring mentioned
is "Honey Spring," about two miles east of Pleasantville, in
Pike county, the place where an Indian fight occurred in 1792.

Since Thomas Freeman was running the lines of the Vincennes tract, in 1802, and passed through this very locality, it is
quite likely that the scout's report referred to Freeman's work.
The division of the land into sections came during and after
1804. Freeman crossed the Indian trail in his survey, and recorded it as 31 miles and 41 chains from the mouth of White
river. Near by was a trappers' coal bank. Freeman recorded
indications of coal at several points near the trail[96] The government surveyors who sub-divided the land within the Freeman lines do not seem to have made any record of the Yellow
Banks trail, but those who worked south of the south Freeman
line made a fairly good record of it almost to Gentryville.
The Rome trace and the Yellow Banks trail joined near the
southwest corner of Dubois county. The government surveyors' records of Ranges 6 and 7, south and west, show this.
They also show where a trace crossed north of Chrisney, not
far from where the remains of Sarah Lincoln Grigsby, the
only sister of Abraham Lincoln, lie buried, in the Old Pigeon
Cemetery.[97]

40

[95] Cockrum's *Pioneer History of Indiana*, pp. 175 and 177.

[96] Miscellaneous Record 1, Indiana, pp. 18 and 19; Executive Journal, Indiana Territory, p. 5; Cockrum's *Pioneer History of Indiana*,
pp. 177 and 178; The "Vincennes tract" was an Indian gift to the
French, Dillon's *Pioneer History of Indiana*, pp. 402 and 403.

[97] Holland's *Lincoln*, p. 38; Monument erected in 1916; Cockrum's
Pioneer History of Indiana, p. 506.

From this Yellow Banks trail, a pioneer road ran from near
Gentryville to the mouth of Anderson river. This might be
called the "Lincoln trace," for it was the route taken by
Thomas Lincoln when he came to Indiana from Kentucky, in
1816.[98] By landing at the mouth of Anderson river and trail-
ing northwest across Spencer county to Lincoln City, Lincoln
shortened his mileage by both water and land. A pioneer road
had been previously cut out for a large part of the way.

Some pioneers who came to Dubois county floated down the
Ohio river to Rockport, followed the Yellow Banks trail to
the Freeman line, then trailed along that line to their Indiana
home.[99]

The Indians used the Yellow Banks trail, or part of it, in
some of their attacks upon white people. The Indians were on
or near the lines leading from their towns on White river to
the Ohio river most of the time in spring, summer and fall
months. In an order issued by General Harrison, on Sunday,
July 12, 1807, he mentions that a band of twelve Indians were
going south from the forks of White river, in such a way as
to strike the Ohio as near as they could at the mouth of Greene
river. Captain Hargrove, to whom the order was addressed,
was on duty on the Buffalo trace. General Harrison said:
"It is hard to determine where they will cross the old Indian
road that you are on, but some place between the Mudhole
[in Dubois county] and the White Oak Springs fort [Peters-
burg]. The people at that fort must be advised. You have the
authority to secure as many men for temporary service from
the White Oak Springs fort as they can spare. You must

41

[98] Holland's *Life of Lincoln,* pp. 25 and 26; The University Society's
Lincoln, Vol. I, p. 24; Herndon & Weik's *Lincoln,* Vol. I, p. 17;
Barrett's *Lincoln,* p. 22; Nicolay's *Lincoln,* p. 7; Cockrum's *Pioneer
History of Indiana,* p. 474; Venable's *"Footprints of Pioneers,"* p. 108.
[99] Rev. Anthony Michel, of Ireland, Indiana.

have the section all along the fifteen miles to the east thoroughly patrolled," etc.[100]   The protection to the east was for the benefit of the McDonald settlement at the Mudhole, south of Portersville, in Dubois county.   The fort mentioned above is still standing at Petersburg, Indiana.   The "Springs" were in section 27, on the old Buffalo trace.[101]

General Harrison in the same order also said: "There will be thirty mounted men from this Post [Vincennes] sent to the south of you who will patrol along and near to the Patoka river, with scouts at the different fords on that river.   With all this vigilance I feel sure that the Indian band will be destroyed or turned back." [102]

These orders established a trail through Pike county from the south, even if not observed or noted by the government surveyors, in 1804.   It may have been a "dry weather trail." Colonel Hargrove and four other men named by the General Assembly of Indiana, on December 21, 1816, to fix a seat of justice for Pike county, on February 15, 1817, made a report selecting Petersburg.   In this report they say: "We would willingly have examined that part of the county south of Patoka had the season and weather admitted of it." [103]

Patoka river seems to have been a natural home of the beaver, an animal very fond of water, and valued by Indians. Even to-day many signs of old beaver dams may be seen.[104]

---

[100] Cockrum's *Pioneer History of Indiana,* pp. 149, 167, 210 and 211.

[101] Plat Book 5, p. 157, State Auditor's Office; Indiana Historical Society's Publication, Vol. 2, p. 131.

[102] Cockrum's *Pioneer History of Indiana,* p. 211.

[103] History of Pike and Dubois Counties, pp. 273, 274 and 336.

[104] Wilson's *History of Dubois County,* p. 86; Cockrum's *Pioneer History of Indiana,* pp. 106, 118, 177 and 444; Smith's *"Early Indiana Trials and Sketches,"* p. 449; Indiana Historical Society's Publications, Vol. 5, pp. 317 and 395; Morris Birkbeck's "Notes," etc., p. 130; Indiana and Indianans, p. 58; Indiana Historical Society's Publications, Vol. 1, p. 126.

Scouts were kept on guard along the Yellow Banks as late
as October 28, 1807. The scout, FuQuay, was one of the
most trusted men in General Harrison's employ.[105]

General Harrison made every effort possible to induce the
misguided followers of Aaron Burr to settle in southern Indiana along these old Indian traces.[106]

A fort or stockade stood near Selvin, in Warrick county,
probably near the junction of the Rome and Yellow Banks
trails. It is likely General Harrison referred to this junction
when he wrote, October 4, 1807, as follows: "This is a very
desirable place to have a strong fort. In making the building
be sure that it is strongly put together, made out of large logs
and that a stockade ten feet high be built that will enclose one
acre of ground. In this enclosure can be erected a number of
strong buildings that will safely protect fifty people. This
will be a rallying point for all who may come later to that
section." Captain Hargrove was collecting Burr refugees and
getting them to settle along the various Indian traces and military roads.[107]

In an advertisement which appeared in the Vincennes Sun
of June 6, 1818, proclaiming the advantages of Rockport and
offering Rockport town lots for sale, Rockport is described as
being on the Ohio river "ten miles above the Yellow Banks."
Captain W. H. Daniel, a well-known Ohio river pilot of Jas-

[105] Cockrum's *Pioneer History of Indiana,* pp. 207 and 223.

[106] Cockrum's *Pioneer History of Indiana,* pp. 176, 213, 216, 217, 218,
219, 471, 472 and 478; Indiana Historical Society's Publications, Vol.
2, pp. 24 and 75.

[107] Cockrum's *Pioneer History of Indiana,* pp. 218, 226 and 472;
Captain Hargrove was born in South Carolina, 1775; History of Gibson County, pp. 51, 154 and 219.

per, always referred to Owensboro, Kentucky, as "Yellow Banks." [108]

When town lots at Portersville were offered for sale, July 20, 1818, by County Agent Niblack through an advertisement in the Vincennes Sun, Portersville was described as being on the main traveled route from Louisville, Corydon, to Vincennes, etc. This would indicate that people came from Corydon either by way of Paoli, and the Buffalo trace, or by way of the military road from Milltown to Enlow's Mill (Jasper), and thence north on the east fork of the Yellow Banks trail to Portersville.[109]

RED BANKS TRAIL.

The left hand bank of the Ohio river at Henderson, Kentucky, was called "Red Banks." A trail led from Evansville to Vincennes and it was called the Red Banks trail.

The inhabitants of Vincennes, in 1800 and again in 1802, petitioned the Senate and House of Representatives of the United States concerning slavery and many other things of vital interest at that time. They asked that a law be enacted so that the governor could grant 400 acres of land to persons he may select, provided they erect "houses of entertainment," and open good wagon roads on the trails leading from Clark's Grant to Vincennes, from Vincennes to Henderson (Kentucky), etc. The "houses of entertainment" (forts or taverns) were not to exceed twenty miles apart. This indicates

---

[108] *Early Travels in Indiana,* p. 27; *Indiana Magazine of History,* Vol. 11, No. 2, June, 1915, p. 104.

[109] Esarey's *Indiana,* pp. 242 and 246; Vincennes Sun, of 1818; Indiana Historical Society's Publications, Vol. 6, pp. 290, 296-297; "Western Sun," see Brown's *Western Gazetteer* (1817), p. 66.

the prominence of the Buffalo trace and the Red Banks trail.[110] This idea was, in a measure, provided for in the treaty of Fort Wayne, 1803.[111]

This old Red Banks trail was patrolled in pioneer days for the protection of settlers coming into Indiana. Captain William Hargrove, under orders from General Harrison, April 20, 1807, had charge of this line of work. His instructions were: "You will divide your force and form a squad of six men under a reliable man who will act as sergeant to patrol the main traveled way from your settlement south to the Ohio river, at Red Banks. Instruct the sergeant to make two trips each way every ten days. I will send a scout who will come with the men and carts that bring the supplies." The governor of Indiana territory granted a license to John A. Miller to conduct a ferry across Patoka river, at what is now Patoka, in Gibson county, on May 23, 1807.[112]

At one time the Indians had a battle with a boat crew at Red Banks, and a son of an Indian who lost his father in the fight had to be carefully guarded against to prevent him from leading an attack upon emigrants.[113] Many of the emigrants that settled in the northern part of Vanderburg county and in the western part of Gibson county came over the Red Banks trail. Major Sprinkles lived on this old trail.[114]

45

110 For Henderson, see decorations, Seelbach Hotel, Louisville; Indiana Historical Society's Publication, Vol. 4, p. 110, Vol. 6, pp. 291 and 296, Vol. 2, pp. 458 and 464.

111 Senate Documents, Vol. 39, pp. 64 and 65; Brown's *"Western Gazetteer,"* pp. 68, 69 and 70.

112 Indiana Historical Society's Publications, Vol. 3, p. 140; Cockrum's *Pioneer History of Indiana,* pp. 204 and 502.

113 Cockrum's *Pioneer History of Indiana,* pp. 156 and 210. (Note: "Red Banks"—in Kentucky, opposite Range 11 west, in Indiana); *Early Travels in Indiana,* pp. 27, 182 to 187, 283.

114 Cockrum's *Pioneer History of Indiana.* p. 220.

46

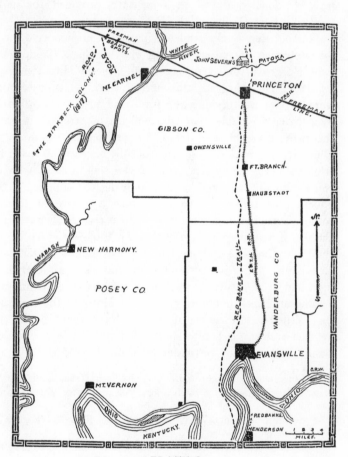

PLATE 8.

The Red Banks trail passed through the environs of Princeton, and a settlement there previous to 1802 caused the Freeman line to be deflected so as to embrace a triangle running from the mouth of White river to a point near the shops of the Southern railroad, thus including the settlements within white territory.[115]   Henderson, Kentucky, was formerly called "Red Banks."

There was an old Indian trail near the Ohio river, in Posey county.   It began in Spencer or Warrick county, and went to the Saline region of Illinois, south of the little Wabash river.   The Shawnees, under Chief Setteedown, had villages along this trail, not far from Newburg, at one time known as Sprinkleburg, a home of Major John Sprinkles.[116]

47

SALT ROUTE OR TRACE.

In General Harrison's treaty with the Indians at Fort Wayne, June 7, 1803, the Vincennes tract was ceded to the United States, by a specific description, using Surveyor Freeman's "calls,"—the first treaty of its kind in Indiana.   In addition, the tribes relinquished and ceded "to the United States the great salt spring upon the Saline creek, which falls into the Ohio below the mouth of the Wabash, with a quantity of land surrounding it, not exceeding four miles

[115] Article 5, Treaty of Fort Wayne, 1803; Senate Documents, Vol. 39, pp. 64 and 65.

[116] Cockrum's *Pioneer History of Indiana*, pp. 220, 502, 503 and 504; *Early Travels in Indiana*, p. 113, 128 and 129, 232, 300-8, 510 and 511, 162, 182, 186, 211, 520; Esarey's *Indiana*, p. 97.   (Note: For a good pioneer description of Princeton and southwestern Indiana, as of 1817, read Morris Birkbeck's *"Notes on a Journey in America,"* published in London, 1818, pp. 89-144.   It also covers the Saline country in Illinois.)

square," etc. The spring was in what is now Illinois, near Shawneetown, named in honor of the most conceited and warlike of the aboriginees.[117]—"the first at the battle, and the last at the treaty."

There was an old traveled way from Vincennes that crossed White river near where Hazleton is, and the Patoka river at John Severns',[118] about three miles north of Princeton, and continued southwest to the Wabash river near the mouth of the Little Wabash, where it crossed the Wabash. The Little Wabash river flows into the Wabash river at the northeast corner of Gallatin county, Illinois, about nine miles north of the mouth of the Wabash, and about fifteen miles north of Shawneetown, Illinois. The Saline springs and salt works were near by, on Saline creek. The route described was known, in 1807, as the "Salt route."[119] Part of the trail was in Illinois. Salt makers at the spring mentioned had to be protected against Indian raids, even though the Indians received 150 bushels of salt annually as their royalty. This salt route, and the guards on duty about the salt works, were mentioned in General Harrison's military orders in September, 1807. In 1750, a stockade fort was built in Indiana, across from these springs. The production of salt at the "United States Saline," twenty-six miles below the mouth of

117 *Ferry,* by Jos. Decker, Jr., Feb. 2, 1803; Indiana Historical Society's Publications, Vol. 3, p. 116; *Early Travels in Indiana,* pp. 38 and 222; Dillon's *Indiana,* p. 103; Esarey's *Indiana,* p. 74; Treaty, Senate Documents, Vol. 39, pp. 64 and 65; (Note: Salt was a valuable commodity in 1804). See the surveyor's description of French Lick Springs, Vol. 2, N. & W., pp. 81 and 82.

118 Note: On May 23, 1807, John A. Miller was licensed by the territorial government "to keep a ferry across the Patoka river" at Patoka ,Indiana.—Indiana Historical Society's Publications, Vol. 3, p. 140.

the Wabash river, reached between 200,000 and 300,000 bushels annually.

The John Severns mentioned above was a very successful "scout" and pathfinder in his day, and rendered valuable service to General Harrison in establishing traces, both blind and blazed traces.[120] Captain Dubois captured three stolen horses from the Indians on this Salt route,[121] in 1813. His name appears to an Indian treaty signed December 30, 1805, for land in Illinois.

There were four east and west traces cut out or improved by white pioneers between the Ohio and White rivers, and four north and south traces between the Wabash and Blue rivers. In this particular work John Severns, a Welshman who lived on Patoka river, northwest of Princeton, was a valuable help. He made the first permanent settlement in

49

[119] Esarey's *Indiana*, p. 97, for White river crossing; Indiana Historical Society's Publication, Vol. 5, p. 413; See Article 3, Treaty of Fort Wayne, June 7, 1803, Senate Documents, Vol. 39, pp. 64 and 65; Esarey's *Indiana*, p. 37; Cockrum's *Pioneer Indiana*, pp. 117, 144, 216, 219, 224, 225, 238, 464 and 474; Old Salt Trail crosses the Wabash just below New Harmony; "*Once Upon a Time in Indiana*," p. 169; "*Notes on a Journey in America*,"—Morris Birkbeck, pp. 101-144. (Note: Birkbeck's Colony is described by Cobbett, in "*Early Travels in Indiana*," pp. 511-513. Morris Birkbeck was an English Quaker farmer of education and ability. His "*Notes*" are highly instructive and full of pioneer information—a record worthy of preservation.) "*Early Travels in Indiana*," p. 171; Brown's *Western Gazetteer* (1817), pp. 26, 50 and 51.

[120] Cockrum's *Pioneer History of Indiana*, pp. 212, 214, 215 and 166.

[121] Dillon's *Indiana*, pp. 55, 57 and 527; Indiana Historical Society's Publication, Vol. 3, p. 186, a note at foot of page; Ellis' *Life of Daniel Boone*, p. 97; Book 49062 Indiana State Library, p. 227; See map in *American Motorist*, December number, 1915; Dillon's *Indiana*, p. 450.

what is now Gibson county. He had been a soldier in the Revolutionary War.

One of these traces left the Red Banks trace at a point probably south of Haubstadt, and went "east parallel with the river from forty to fifty miles." This crossed the Rome trace, and went toward Fredonia. It was near William Rector's "base line," which was 24 miles south of the Buckingham Base Line, the basis of Indiana surveys.[122] There was also one that ran south of Patoka and across the Yellow Banks trail to the Blue river trace.[123] The Buffalo trace, in Dubois county, was improved by General Harrison, by cutting out shorter routes, and for that reason it is known in places as the Governor's trace, or Harrison's road.[124] There was also a trace cut out from near Otwell east by way of Jasper to the Blue river at Milltown, or near there.

In an order written November 4, 1807, General Harrison said to Captain William Hargrove: "You now have four roads or traces running to the east that can be easily found and traveled over, dividing your territory into sections between the Ohio and White rivers."[125] The main routes were the Buffalo trace, Patoka river trace, Haubstadt trace, and the Rome trace. These with their branches formed a means of travel east and west.

In the same order General Harrison wrote: "Also you have four roads or traces running north and south dividing your territory in that direction from near the Wabash on the west to Blue river on the east, thus enabling you to give much better protection to settlers now there and to the emigrants coming into your territory," etc.

[122] Indiana Historical Society's Publication, Vol. 3, p. 192.
[123] Cockrum's *Pioneer History of Indiana,* pp. 165, 166, 168, 214 and 215.
[124] Wilson's *History of Dubois County,* pp. 27, 31 and 74.
[125] Cockrum's *Pioneer History of Indiana,* p. 224.

50

The systematic and military tact of General Harrison is apparent. The four main north and south routes were Blue river, Yellow Banks (two branches), Red Banks and the Salt route. The Rome trace also may have been considered in this group.

WHETZEL'S TRACE.

A trace that at once sprung into use was the Whetzel trace through the New Purchase. It appears that in 1817, Jacob Whetzel selected a tract of land in the Harrison Purchase, about Worthington, at the mouth of Eel river (before the treaty of Saint Mary's, October 2-6, 1818), and that his home was near Laurel, on the Whitewater river, in Franklin county. To go from his home to his Eel river location by water would require a long voyage, part of it up stream. To avoid this he resolved to cut a trace across the Indian lands then about to become the New Purchase. In doing so his trace covered a distance of over sixty miles through a primeval forest. He struck the west fork of White river at the site of Waverly, five miles north of a point sixty miles west of Laurel, thus he traveled west on an angle of only 4° 45' 48" from Laurel,—a remarkable achievement for a woodsman in his day, provided he really intended to travel due west of Laurel. The location attracted his fancy to such an extent that he resolved to make it a habitation and a home, thus his settlement and the New Purchase treaty bear almost the same date. The Waverly settlement took the place of his Eel river enterprise. Had he floated down White river he would not have reached the Harrison Purchase until he passed under the Ten-O'clock Line at Gosport.

Before Jacob Whetzel undertook to cut a trace to the west

fork of White river he took the precaution to get permission
from the Indians. In the summer of 1818, Jacob Whetzel
visited Chief Anderson, of the Delaware Indians, whose home
was near the site of Anderson, Indiana, and obtained permission to cut the trace. In Whetzel's party were his son
Cyrus, a youth of eighteen; Thomas Howe, Thomas Rush,
Richard Rush and Walter Banks.

Jacob Whetzel and Thomas Rush selected the route, perhaps guided by a hand compass, and occasionally by an Indian
trail. The other men cut out the route wide enough for the
passage of a team. The trace ran about seven miles below
the present site of Rushville, four miles above Shelbyville,
and a little north of Boggstown. The road soon became
known as "Whetzel's Trace." These pioneers gave names to
many creeks as they cut out the trace. The trace proved to
be of great importance in the settlement of Marion, Johnson,
Morgan and Shelby counties. The boy Cyrus became a pioneer surveyor and surveyed the "bluff road" from Waverly
to Franklin. The road was cut out in 1824. The name
"bluffs" was given to the White river hills in Morgan county
by Jacob Whetzel. In cutting out their trace the Whetzel
party had no thought of making a road for subsequent travel.
It was intended only for the Whetzel teams, on their way to
White river, but it soon became a line of general travel.

The son, Cyrus Whetzel, is recorded as probably the first
settler of Morgan county, though his land entry bears date
of July 17, 1821. He could not purchase it until the surveys
of his range were completed and the land opened for entry.
The surveys were made in September, 1820, by John Mc-
Donald, who surveyed the "Ten O'Clock Line," and B. Bently,
both government deputy surveyors. Cyrus Whetzel was born
in Ohio county, Virginia, December 1, 1800, and entered his
land before he was twenty-one. He was elected to the house
of representatives in 1858, and was probably the foremost

backwoodsman of the general assembly of Indiana. From 1827 to 1862 he operated a ferry across White river, near his home. He died December 16, 1871. Jacob Whetzel, the father, found delight in hunting and trapping about Waverly until the end of his days. The prominence that came to Whetzel's trace was due to the fact that it was the earliest east and west road through the New Purchase. There was an old Indian trail from the south. These two traces soon became main lines of travel. Many pioneers from Ohio and Kentucky entered land in the same township, the same day Cyrus Whetzel did, which was upon the opening of the public sale of land in his range, for his land district, Brookville, afterward known as the Indianapolis Land Office District. Cyrus Whetzel first bought 137.14 acres, on the south side of White river in section 23, near what is now Waverly. White river ran almost due west past his land. Later he made other entries.[126]

In all these traces, trails, routes, pioneer roads, etc., the making of a state became possible, and for that reason they are worthy of study and consideration. When General Harrison came to Vincennes his principal work was to establish roads and houses of accommodation between the settlements, fix the boundaries of the old Vincennes Tract and Kaskaskia Grant, make provision for the security of traders in the Indian country,[127] etc. He did so, created a state, and found his way to the White House.

53

[126] Brown's *"Western Gazetteer"* (1817), p. 71 (p. 358, Eel River); Indiana Historical Society's Publications, Vol. 2, page 34, Vol. 4, p. 313. Vol. 5, pp. 240, 242, 423 and 454; Esarey's *Indiana*, p. 243; Banta's *History of Johnson County*, pp. 9-14, 17 and 117; *Brant and Fuller's History of Johnson County*, pp. 293-297; Plat Book 3, p. 4, Vol, 12, pp. 337-351 N. & E.; Tract Book 1, pp. 261-267, Indianapolis District (at office of Auditor of State).

[127] Indiana Historical Society's Publications, Vol. 4 ,p. 253; *Early Travels in Indiana*, p. 232.

54

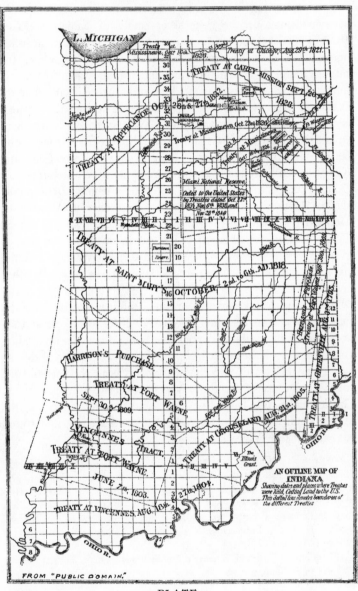

PLATE 9.

PART II.

————

PIONEER SURVEYING IN INDIANA.

————

This article is intended to serve only as an introduction to a neglected field of interesting information. No attempt is made to cover all the Indiana surveys, or any one survey completely. Typical cases, or cases more or less historical, have been selected with a view of showing how vast is the field of information to be found in the old official survey records, provided he who searches understands something about surveyors' field notes, their terms, abbreviations, etc., and can, in a measure, convert them into common language, and re-locate his findings on an ordinary map. As far as possible, technical terms and professional formula have been eliminated in this article. The authority quoted, so far as written records are concerned, refers to the state field notes and maps in the office of the Auditor of State, of the state of Indiana. Other references explain themselves.

There were several old surveys in Indiana before the Indian title was extinguished, namely, the French tracts at Vincennes, Clark's grant in Clark and Scott counties, etc. As title came to the government the rectangular system of surveys was put into effect, running up to and touching the old surveys. In this way the old surveys are located upon the maps. The survey system, as used in Indiana, was ordered by congress, and for that reason we often hear of a "congressional township."

The line dividing the states of Ohio and Indiana is known

55

as the first principal meridian. This line coincides with 84° 51' west of Greenwich. This meridian governs Indiana lands east of the Greenville treaty line, a line agreed upon August 3, 1795.

The range line that starts at the confluence of the Little Blue river with the Ohio and runs to the northern boundary of Indiana, was named the SECOND PRINCIPAL ME-RIDIAN, and governs the surveys of all public lands in Indiana, except those mentioned above. It "coincides" with 86° 28' west longitude. The base line crosses this at right angles, at 38° 28' 20'' north latitude. From these two lines all of the later rectangular work takes its name and number. These will be more fully considered hereinafter.

Fairly complete instructions, rules and regulations were given to the deputy surveyors who were to subdivide Ohio and Indiana into townships and sections. Among pages of instructions are the following: "You will be careful to note in your field book * * * all rivers, creeks, springs and smaller streams of water, with their width and the course they run in crossing the lines of survey, and whether navigable, rapid, or mountainous, the kinds of timber and undergrowth with which the land may be covered, all swamps, ponds, stone quarries, coal beds, peat or turf grounds, uncommon, natural or artificial productions, such as mounds, precipices, caves, etc., all rapids, cascades or falls of water, materials, ores, fossils, etc.; the quality of the soil and the true situation of all mines, salt-licks, salt-springs and mill seats, which may come to your knowledge."[128] The foregoing in-

128 Booklet, *"The Public Domain and its Survey,"* 1892; Official Records and Original Field Notes; Indiana Historical Society's Publications, Vol. 4, pp. 98, 110 and 254, Vol. 1, p. 126; "Indiana and Indianans," p. 58, for "trees of peace"; The Public Domain, Vol. 19, p. 180.

structions were followed in Indiana as soon as the rectangular system of surveys were begun. However, before that time several important surveys were made. The most important were the surveys of Clark's Grant, the Greenville treaty line, and the Vincennes tract. These deserve separate mention, bcause each is typical of its kind.

SURVEYS MADE PREVIOUS TO THE GENERAL SURVEY OF INDIANA.

THE ILLINOIS OR CLARK'S GRANT.

By the provisions of an act of the General Assembly of Virginia, of the 3rd of October, 1779, and the 5th of October, 1780, the following land bounties were promised to the officers and soldiers of Virginia who served to the end of the Revolutionary War, viz: To a major general, 15,000 acres; to a brigadier general, 10,000 acres; to a colonel, 6,666 2/3 acres; to a lieutenant colonel, 6,000 acres; to a major, 5,666 2/3 acres; to a captain, 4,000 acres; to a subaltern, 2,66 2/3 acres; to a non-commissioned officer, 400 acres, and to a private, 200 acres.

A grant had been given to General George Rogers Clark, and to the officers and soldiers of his regiment, that had marched with him when the posts of Kaskaskia and Vincennes were reduced, and to the officers and soldiers that had been since incorporated into the said regiment.

In 1786, the reservation was laid off on the borders of the Ohio river, adjacent to the falls, by William Clark, a surveyor, and a cousin of General George Rogers Clark. The commissioners who were selected to sign the deeds of allotments were,—William Clark, William Croghan, Abraham

Chaplain, Richard Taylor, Alexander Breckenridge, Richard Terrell, James Francis Moore and Andrew Heth.

In those days a grant of land was usually laid out at right angles to a stream of water, so Clark's Grant took its general boundary lines from the trend of the Ohio river at Eighteen-Mile-Island, northeast of Louisville, Kentucky. The survey map of the Illinois Grant shows "a dense cane brake" existed north of the Six-Mile-Island, in 1796. It was north of the present site of Clarksville and between Silver creek and the Ohio river. The record of the survey, as originally made, differs about five degrees from that made by the government deputy surveyors at a later date. Evidently Surveyor William Clark did not allow for the magnetic variation. His survey could be correct without it. The rectangular system of surveys was adopted May 20, 1785, but the outlines of Clark's Grant did not call for it. In 1795, the Indians relinquished their title to the land in Clark's Grant by the treaty of Greenville.

The patent for Clark's Grant bears date of December 14, 1786. It reads as follows:

"Edmund Randolph, Esquire, Governor of the Commonwealth of Virginia,—

"To all to whom these presents shall come, Greeting:

"Know ye, that by virtue of an act of Assembly passed in the October Session, 1783, entitled an act for surveying the lands granted to the Illinois Regiment, and establishing a town within the said grant, there is granted by the said Commonwealth unto William Fleming, John Edwards, John Campbell, George Rogers Clark, John Montgomery, Abraham Chaplain, John Bailey, Robert Todd, William Clark, James Francis Moore, Alexander Breckenridge, Robert Breckenridge, Richard Taylor, Andrew Heth, Richard Terrell and William Croghan, as a board of commissioners to and for

58

the uses and purposes expressed in the said act a certain tract
or parcel of land containing one hundred and forty-nine thousand acres, lying and being on the northwest side of the Ohio
river and bounded as follows, to-wit:

"BEGINNING at a white oak, blue ash and hickory nearly
opposite the upper point of the Eighteen-Mile-Island on
the bank of the river,

RUNNING N. 40° W. 4652 poles, crossing Fourteen-Mile-
Creek three times, and sundry branches, to a black gum,
white oak and sugar tree.

THENCE S. 50° W. 1006 [or 1600] poles to three white
oaks,

THENCE S. 40° E. 300 poles to three white oaks,

THENCE S. 50° W. 1866 poles to two black oaks and a
Spanish oak near the Knobs.

THENCE S. 40° E. 300 poles to a poplar, white oak and
dogwood,

THENCE S. 50° W. 533 poles to three white oaks on the
point of a ridge,

THENCE S. 40° E. 600 poles to a poplar, beech and ash,

THENCE S. 50° W. 533 poles to three white oaks and dogwood sapling,

THENCE S. 40° E. 1200 poles, crossing the muddy fork
of Silver Creek three times, to a white oak and two dogwood saplings,

THENCE S. 2° W. 2840 poles to two elms and a beech
on the bank of Falling Run,

THENCE S. 40° E. crossing said run, 320 poles to the
Ohio, a poplar and two beeches,

THENCE up the river, as it meanders 340 poles to a small
white thorn, white oak and hickory near the mouth of Silver Creek, and corner to the one thousand acres laid off
agreeable to the aforesaid act for a town,

59

THENCE with the lines thereof N. 170 poles, crossing Silver Creek twice to a sweet gum, beech and sugar tree,

THENCE E. 326 poles, crossing the creek to three beeches,

THENCE S. 40° E. 86 poles to a beech and sugar,

THENCE E. 176 poles to a large sweet gum, dogwood and sugar tree,

THENCE S. 180 poles to a sugar and two white ash trees,

THENCE — 158 poles to three beeches,

THENCE S. 280 poles to two white ashes and hickory on the Ohio,

THENCE up the same, with its meanderings, to the beginning," etc., etc.

There were 1,000 acres in the Clarksville grant and 149,000 in the main grant. This survey is treated somewhat in full, because it is typical of the plans of surveys usual in the days before the rectangular systems of surveys were put into effect. The tract may be observed on any large map of Indiana, and most of it is now within the boundaries of Clark county. It was no small task to divide the tract into allotments. Many contained 500 acres each. For its day the survey was very good, but the description would be more definitely made at the present time. In place of naming a cluster of trees for a corner, their sizes and their directions and distances from the corner post would be mentioned.

Later surveyors who put into effect the rectangular system in Indiana, measured their lines up to the lines of Clark's Grant, thus Clark's Grant is held in position, by its own lines and by those of subsequent surveys, somewhat like a keystone in an arch. There are many such irregular plots in Gibson, Pike, Knox, Daviess, Sullivan and other counties, due to early grants or early acquired titles. These irregular plots of ground prove the value of the rectangular system subsequently adopted.[129]

RE-SURVEY OF THE GREENVILLE TREATY LINE, IN 1800,— THE GORE OF INDIANA.

The Ohio Enabling act of April 30, 1802, gave to Indiana the "gore of Indiana." The western boundary line of the land ceded by the Indians in the treaty of Greenville, August 3, 1795, was designated in the treaty as a line extending from Fort Recovery (Ohio), "southwesterly in a direct line to the Ohio, so as to intersect that river opposite the mouth of the Kentucky or Cuttawa River." Extend the west line of Dearborn county to the Ohio river and to the Ohio state line and you thus locate the Greenville treaty line through Indiana. That part of Indiana east of this line is often referred to as the "gore of Indiana." At one time all of it was known as Dearborn county. The citizens of the "gore" were partial to Ohio.

The record of a re-survey of the "gore line" in Indiana, begins as follows: "Commenced at a maple 10 inches in diameter, standing on the north bank of the Ohio, at a point opposite the mouth of Kentucky river, September 17, 1800; course N. 5° 25' E." This line ran from the above tree to Fort Recovery, Ohio. The tree mentioned is near Lamb, in

61

---

[129] Dillon's *History of Indiana*, pp. 180, 181, 396 and 612; Public Domain, Vol. 19, pp. 171 and 179; Miscellaneous Record No. 1, pp. 1, 2 and 3, and Map of Illinois Grant at State Auditor's Office; Esarey's *Indiana*, pp. 68, 69, 94 and 203; Indiana Historical Society's Publications, Vol. 3, p. 91 (note 3); English's *"Conquest of the Northwest,"* p. 1015; Brown's *"Western Gazetteer"* (1817), p. 78.

the southwest corner of Switzerland county.[130] This surveyor frequently wrote these words in his field notes: "rose
a hill" (meaning that he went up a hill), "rose a rill," "rose
a ridge," etc. While in the neighborhood of Loughery creek
he made this entry: "When on Loughery creek I got my
compass bent by a fall and got another which I know to be
affected by the severe frost. I have now got my former one
righted, but owing to the advanced season and severity of the
weather I find it impossible to run them [the lines] on."[131]
He was engaged in sub-dividing the land east of the Greenville treaty line, i. e., in Dearborn county, etc. This treaty
line was originally surveyed, in 1798, by Israel Ludlow. The
sub-division of the land east of this line belongs to the Ohio
system.

62

THE VINCENNES TRACT, FREEMAN LINES, BUCKINGHAM'S
BASE LINE, AND SECOND PRINCIPAL MERIDIAN.

The story of how there came to be a tract of land known
as the "Vincennes Tract," with its Indian, French and English associations, wars, treaties and settlements, and their
bearing upon the history and surveys of Indiana, constitutes
very interesting reading, dating back almost two hundred
years. Suffice it to say, that in 1742, the Indians gave to the
French, at Vincennes, by means of a "Gift Deed," a tract of

130 *Early Travels in Indiana*, pp. 37, 233 and 461; Record III, West
of First Meridian, p. 96; Indiana Historical Society's Publications, Vol.
2, p. 492, Vol. 3, pp. 65, 67 and 116; Dillon's *History of Indiana*, pp.
609, 610, 333, 357, 358 and 374.

131 Indiana Historical Society's Publications, Vol. 2, pp. 366 and 492,
Vol. 4, p. 307, Vol. 1, pp. 136, 329, 335, 345, 351, 352, 363 and 364; Rec-
ord III, West of First Meridian, p. 106; Venable's *"Footprints of the
Pioneers,"* p. 55.

land lying at right angles to the general trend of the Wabash river at Vincennes. In 1763 the English conquered it from the French, and in 1779 General Clark captured it from the English in his conquest of the Northwest Territory, so from this date we begin.

Draw a line on a state map, from Orleans, in Orange county, to Point Coupee,[132] on the Wabash river, and you will have the north line of that part of the Vincennes Tract which is in Indiana. Run the line from Orleans to a point seven and one-half miles south of the southeast corner of Dubois county, where Dubois, Crawford and Perry unite, and you will locate the southeast corner of the Vincennes Tract. Draw a line thence to the mouth of White river, and you will have the south line of the Vincennes Tract, so far as Indiana is concerned. These lines and corners are locally known by the name of "Freeman." The Vincennes Tract contained about 1,600,000 acres. The survey began in the summer or fall of 1802, and was not completed until in 1803. The north line started at Point Coupee, near Merom, in Sullivan county, and ran south 78° east, passed near Odon, and ended in section 19, near Orleans, at what is known as "Freeman's Corner." His field notes are not altogether dry reading. He recorded Indian trails, crab orchards, very large springs, trees, rivers, etc. The corner near Orleans is 57 miles due east of Vincennes. From Orleans the line runs south 12° west 40 miles, and passes near Paoli, Eckerty, etc. There are many interesting items mentioned in his record, but they must be omitted here.

In the survey of the south line he began at the mouth of White river and ran south 78° east, 59 miles to a point in

63

[132] August 20, 1729; Indiana Historical Society's Publications, Vol. 3, p. 294.

Perry county. Near this line is Princeton, Oakland City, Holland, St. Meinrad, etc. In the survey at Princeton he made an offset, in order to keep Princeton within the treaty territory, a privilege he had under a later treaty. Occasionally along his lines a sapling was split by Freeman's men, and a limb returned through the body, thus a line of "peace trees" was established. In time, the sapling grew to be a deformed forest tree, and did its part to preserve the location of the line. Some people who have lived near the line recall such trees on their farms.[133]

Enough has been mentioned to show how well the work was done. It seems that Surveyor Freeman took an "exception" mentioned in the Wabash Land Company's deed, and "Exception 2" in the Greenville treaty, and by a survey produced a description of the Vincennes Tract by metes and bounds, which was used when a new treaty was made at Fort Wayne, June 7, 1803. It appears that when Freeman had about completed his survey, a new Indian treaty was made, and in this treaty a very definite description was used, thus clearing away any cloud that may have been upon the title and description. In other words, the government went back of all French and English deeds or treaties, and again bought direct from the Indians, who were the remote owners. In this treaty the boundaries, as established by Surveyor Freeman, were agreed upon.

As soon as this treaty had been signed, settlers began to drift toward Vincennes, with a view of making a home on the land. Surveyors were put to work to survey the Vincennes Tract into townships and sections. The base line passes east and west almost near its center. The second principal meridian practically passes through the "Freeman Cor-

[133] See Indiana Historical Society's Publications, Vol. 1, p. 126, and Indiana and Indianans, p. 58.

ner" at Orleans. Surveyors had contracts to survey the tract by ranges six miles wide, running north and south from Freeman line to Freeman line; thus settlements and surveys made a forward move. Before long a land office was established at Vincennes, and land was open for entry.

We, who live in Indiana, do not appreciate our rectangular system of surveys as we should. The system is a blessing, and saves endless litigation. Kentucky had no such system, and many of its worthy pioneers lost their lands for want of a survey. Thomas Lincoln left Kentucky because he was not sure of his title. Daniel Boone, Kentucky's star pioneer, and hundreds of other Kentucky pioneers, were victims of defective land titles. The lessons learned in Kentucky caused many to come to Indiana.

Travelers entered the Vincennes Tract by way of the Buffalo Trace from Louisville; the Rome Trace, or Rome Road, from Rome, in Perry county, via Fulda, Mariah Hill, Selvin, etc.; the Yellow Banks Trace, by way of Rockport, Selvin, etc.; The Red Banks Trace, by way of Henderson, Evansville, Priceton, etc.; and the Shawnee Trace in Illinois. These towns are mentioned to serve as guides. Not all were known then, or even contemplated.

It is plain to be seen that in order to get into the Vincennes Tract the settlers had to travel over Indian land, and General Harrison began to negotiate with the Indians for the land between the Vincennes Tract and the Ohio river. He met with pronounced success. By a treaty at Vincennes, in August, 1804, the Indians ceded the land in Indiana that lies south of the old Buffalo Trace, and the Vincennes Tract to the United States. This second treaty was signed at Vincennes, in August, 1804, and surveyors were put to work to block out the new land into sections. No doubt this second purchase caused the second principal meridian to be moved twelve miles east from where it was originally intended to be, to where it is today.

Who was Thomas Freeman? It must be recalled that Florida was a Spanish possession. On October 27, 1795, a treaty was made between the United States and Spain, defining the boundaries of these countries in the south and west, about Florida, and at 31° north latitude on the Mississippi, etc. The treaty was ratified March 3, 1796, and on May 24, 1796, Thomas Freeman was appointed surveyor, on the part of the United States, for the purpose of running the national boundary line mentioned in said treaty. It thus appears that Thomas Freeman must have been a surveyor that enjoyed the confidence of his country, and had had unusual experience before he came to Indiana. From 1820 to 1822 he was surveyor-general of the public domain south of the state of Tennessee.[134]

Ebenezer Buckingham, Jr., surveyed the base line, in 1804. In surveying the base line, he started in Illinois at a point on the Freeman line on the south side of the Vincennes Tract, and ran east. At 67½ miles he set a post, which, in time, proved to be 3.60 chains west of the present line between Dubois and Orange counties, and which will be referred to again. He marked "line trees," kept a record, drove "mile" and "half mile" posts, but he was "just running an east and west line, without establishing any corners."

On October 15, 1804, he began at the southeast corner of the Vincennes Tract, as located by Thomas Freeman, and ran a line due north (which line is now recognized as the east line of Dubois county), until he struck his base line, on what is now the line between Dubois and Orange counties, and at a point 67 miles and 43.60 chains east of where he started,

134 "The Public Domain," Vol. 19, p. 171.

and 3.60 chains east of a half mile post. As he found it, the line from the southeast corner of the Vincennes Tract to the base line is 22 miles and 44.50 chains long. Having intersected his base line at a point due north of the southeast Freeman corner, he proceeded east on the base line, marking "section corners," and "half section corners," and corner witness trees, and recording them as he went, until he reached the Freeman line on the east end of the Vincennes Tract, at 7 miles and 50.30 chains east of the Dubois and Orange county line. Then he came back to the "initial corner," on the "county line," and went west on his base line, marking each "section corner," "half section corner," and recording corner witness trees, until he was back into Illinois and struck the south Freeman line again, at a point 43.60 chains west of the northeast corner of Section 2, Township 1, South Range 14 West, which was his starting point. As he went west he probably reset all his "mile posts" and "half mile posts," east 3.60 chains, and made them section and half section corner posts, in order to adjust them to the line he ran north from Freeman's corner in what is now Perry county. He reversed his base line and thus threw the 3.60 chains on the Freeman line in Illinois, thus showing that he regarded the crossing at the Orange and Dubois county line as his "initial point."

This brings out a point of unusual interest. In southern Indiana, sections were first numbered, under our rectangular survey system, where the base line crosses the county line between Orange and Dubois counties. "Until this point was found Buckingham did not use the term 'section.'" Evidently the intention was to make the east line of Dubois county the line of the "Second Principal Meridian," which was to start north from the southeast corner of the Vincennes Tract, for he ran that line north "just as a line." Later, surveyors began on the base line and re-marked the

67

68

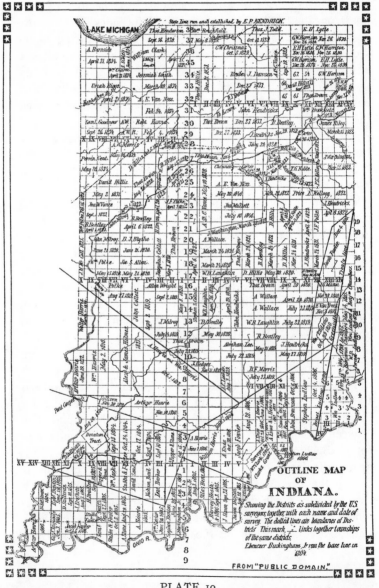

OUTLINE MAP
OF
INDIANA.

Showing the Districts as subdivided by the U.S.
surveyors, together with each name and date of
survey. The dotted lines are boundaries of Districts. This mark, ⌐ ⌐ Links together townships
of the same districts.
Ebenezer Buckingham, Jr ran the base line in
1804.

FROM "PUBLIC DOMAIN."

PLATE 10.

meridian line south, marking section and half section corners and recording witness trees, and numbering them from the base line south as they went.

In surveying what is now the east line of Dubois county for a meridian line, Mr. Buckingham made this record:

"Beginning with the MERIDIAN LINE at the southeast corner of the Vincennes Tract, as established by Mr. Freeman," etc.

In September, 1805, Buckingham extended his base line east from the Vincennes Tract to a point twelve miles from the Dubois and Orange county line, and then ran NORTH to the north line of the VINCENNES TREATY line of August, 1804, which had been surveyed from the Vincennes Tract to Clark's grant, in July, 1805, by William Rector. This last north and south line was finally selected and named the SECOND PRINCIPAL MERIDIAN. It extends from the Ohio river to the state of Michigan, etc.; thus, after all, the southeast Freeman corner controlled and, finally, really located the present well-known "second principal meridian," which coincides with 86° 28′ west of Greenwich, England, This line happens to be where it is, because it is twelve miles east of the southeast corner of the Vincennes Tract. At the time Buckingham contracted to do the work a meridian line could not have been run from the northeast Freeman corner, for the reason that the very moment he moved north or south of the corner he would have been on Indian ground. The base line coincides with 38° 28′ 20″ north latitude.

When Buckingham came north from the Freeman corner, in what is now Perry county, and intersected his base line, he recorded two "BEECH TREES" as witness trees, and thus a system began. These same trees are the witness trees at the corner of four congressional townships, and thus two beech trees, both north of the base line, one in Dubois county and one in Orange county, are the first witness trees on record in connection with a township corner in the very extensive surveys governed by this great base line and second principal meridian. Both of these two great lines were primarily extended from the Freeman lines. It is probable that these two lines are ordinary section lines dignified with the names *Base Line* and *Second Principal Meridian*. From these two lines, the new possessions of the United States were divided into townships and sections, and a new state was born, now known as Indiana. It is easy to see that the Vincennes Tract was the "cradle of the land surveys" of Indiana.

The old original musty field notes, as written on the ground, or at the camps of these pioneer surveyors, are interesting documents to any man who has followed the lines called for by them, found many of the identical trees therein described, and placed his transit over the very "posts" called for by these fading documents. Most of the note books are about three inches by six, made by hand out of old-fashioned "foolscap" paper, sewed together with thread as awkwardly as a man could do it, or tied together with buckskin, cut as thin as a pioneer could do the work. They show the result of perspiration, or snow and rain, pocket wear, and the cruel hand of time; yet they tell a story of pioneer life, no courts or jury ever set aside.

One can easily imagine Thomas Freeman at his work. We can see him with his Jacob-staff in his right hand, his compass swung on his left shoulder, and on his right hip his buckskin pouch, swinging from its shoulder strap, containing his instructions, papers, field notes; an ink-horn, opened at the smaller end, containing "home-made" ink brewed from forest bark; another horn, opened at the larger end, containing dry sand, which he used in his tent, as a blotter is used now; a dozen or more wild goose feathers, from which to make quill pens, etc. With him were his axe-men, "blazers," chainmen, and in the lead a "flagman," wearing a red flannel shirt that he might be more easily seen. He may have been on horseback, and without a flag, or rod. Freeman's cooks, tent men, hunters, and camp-followers were near by. A few "wise chiefs," provided for under the Greenville treaty of 1795, and their dusky warriors may have completed the party. It was not a large party, for Freeman's record speaks of a "little party." Pack horses, with provisions, medicines, and the Kentucky "cure for snake bites" were in charge of the farriers or teamsters.

The white men wore buckskin trousers, raccoon skin caps, moccasins, and the other usual pioneer clothing. The guards or hunters carried their long trusty flint-lock Kentucky or Tennessee rifles, and knew how to hit EITHER eye of a deer, buffalo, or even a squirrel. Wild game or fowl furnished the fresh meat, and perhaps the streams a few fish. Flint, steel, and "punk" supplied fires, and thus the party slowly, but surely, blazed its way over creeks, rivers, valleys and hills; through briers, thickets, barrens, woods, snow and water, opening up a way for those of us who came after them.

Two years after Freeman made his surveys, we find Buckingham, THE BASE LINE AND MERIDIAN LINE SURVEYOR, running a line east and west about the center of the Vincennes Tract, and then going to the Freeman corner, in what is now Perry county, to run a line that struck the base line "on the square," and then and there put into force the great rectangular survey system of the Northwest Territory. His help and party were similar to that we imagine Freeman had. In the final analysis the Freeman line is the hypotenuse of a right angle triangle of which the present

71

base line and the temporary meridian line are the other
factors.

Nothing the writer has ever done has afforded him so much
pleasure as he found, in his boyhood days, when he carried a
transit over the old hills of Dubois county and re-traced these
old lines and re-established some of these old corners. There
was a taste of romance about it, to say the least.

SPECIAL NOTES AND REFERENCES ON THE VINCENNES TRACT
SURVEY AND THE FREEMAN LINES.

Thomas Freeman made the survey of the boundary line of
the Vincennes Tract.[135] The northwest corner of this land
is in Illinois. At a point 21 miles and 110 rods south 12°
west of this corner he crossed the famous "Illinois Trace."[136]
At a point 4 miles and 82 rods north, 78° west of the mouth
of White river, and also in Illinois, he found a "Handsome
Spot."[137] At 5 miles and 50 rods he found a "most beautiful
place." He did not record an Indian trail near here, but
later surveys record two "roads" leading to these two beauty
spots.[138] There was a settlement at Princeton before this
survey was made, so he was permitted to make a triangular
offset in order to include Princeton in the Vincennes
Tract.[139] About 4 miles east of Princeton he recorded an

135 *Early Travels in Indiana,* p. 16; Indiana Historical Society's Publications, Vol. 4, pp. 254 and 255.

136 Miscellaneous Record I, p. 10.

137 Miscellaneous Record I, p. 13.

138 Plat Book V, p. 87. See *"Notes on a Journey in America,"* by
Morris Birkbeck, published in London, 1818, pp. 114-144. A very good
description of "The Birkbeck Colony."

139 Miscellaneous Record I, p. 17; *Early Travels in Indiana,* pp. 27,
113, 129, 186, 283, 437 and 510.

"Indian trace." It was 13¼ miles from the mouth of White river. The longer boundary lines ran south 78° east; the others at right angles to this.[140]

He started to survey the north line of this tract, in Indiana, February 1, 1803, but on account of weather conditions had to wait until February 14, 1803. He crossed the west fork of White river at a point south 78° east of Point Coupee, and a little over 20 miles distant. On this line he located several Indian trails indicating roads to Vincennes, or to Trinity or Indian Springs.[141] About 42 miles from the Wabash on this line he recorded "a large mineral spring at the foot of a hill, spouting in two large streams from a free-stone bottom." This is where the Freeman line crosses a small river above Shoals, in Martin county.[142] Near Huron, and near the county line between Martin and Lawrence counties, Freeman found an oak tree 26 links (over a rod) in circumference. The tree was 5½ feet in diameter.[143] The northeast corner of this tract is near Orleans, nearly one-half mile east of the second principal meridian line. The Grouseland treaty line starts from this corner, and goes toward Brookville, Indiana.[144] In surveying south 12° west from Orleans, Freeman crossed several "trails" and made a record of them. The Buffalo trail or trace, and a trace from Cincinnati unite just west of this line.[145] About three months after the treaty of Fort Wayne was signed Freeman surveyed around the Busseron settlements, beginning on Saturday, September 17, 1803. In a small prairie 3½ miles off the original line he

73

[140] Miscellaneous Record I, p. 17.
[141] Plat Book 2, p. 55.
[142] Miscellaneous Record I, pp. 23-27.
[143] Miscellaneous Record I, p. 27.
[144] Plat Book I, p. 120.
[145] Miscellaneous Record I, p. 29.

marked a black oak "U. S."[146]   He recorded Indian trails here, running north and south.   The Carlisle settlement is recognized in this offset.   The tract was 3½ miles by 5½. A treaty covered this annexation to the Vincennes Tract.[147] Many writers and travelers previous to 1830, recorded wonderful stories about visionary forms of colonies in this locality.

The southeast corner of the Vincennes Tract is in Perry county, 43 chains south of the northeast corner of section 25, township 4 south, range 3 west.   The corner was marked by two beech trees; one 8 inches in diameter stood south 56° east 14 links distant, and the other 7 inches in diameter stood south 88° west 12 links distant.   They were marked by Levi Barber, the surveyor of range 3 west.[148]

74

In Dubois county three handsome markers were erected on the Freeman line, in 1916, as a part of that county's centennial observations.   Two of the markers are on the "French Lick Route" of the Market Highway system, and one is southwest of Holland.

SURVEY OF THE BUFFALO TRAIL.

There was a Buffalo trail, made into a trace, that led from the Falls of the Ohio, through the Vincennes Tract to Vincennes.   The white men held Clark's Grant and the Vincennes Tract, but the trail between the two was on Indian land.   The land south of this trail was purchased from the Indians at Vincennes, August 18 and 27, 1804.   The treaty

146 Miscellaneous Record I, pp. 33 and 34; *Early Travels in Indiana,* pp. 71, 211 and 451.

147 Miscellaneous Record I, p. 34.

148 Record 4, South Range 3 West, p. 107.

reads: "Article VI. As the road from Vincennes to Clark's Grant will form a very inconvenient boundary, and as it is the intention of the parties to these presents, that the whole of the said road shall be within the tract ceded to the United States, it is agreed that the boundary in that quarter shall be a straight line, to be drawn parallel to the course of said road, from the eastern boundary of the tract ceded by the treaty of Fort Wayne, to Clark's grant, but the said line is not to pass at a greater distance than half a mile from the most northerly bend of said road."[149] Of course this was all General Harrison wished. It gave him possession of the trace from the Ohio river to Vincennes. A surveyor was put to work. He surveyed the actual trace by magnetic courses and measured distances, and thus ascertained his final course and ran the boundary line one-half mile from the trail's most northerly bend. His record definitely locates the trail to the Vincennes Trace, and from there to Vincennes the range surveyors noted it in their surveys, thus this old trail is a matter of exact record. The survey of this Buffalo trail, where it was used in the treaty, was made by William Rector. The distance was 40 miles and 42 chains. The work was done in July, 1805. The New Albany and Paoli pike is north of this line.[150] This Buffalo trace or trail is referred to on early maps as "Buffalo Trace," "Kentucky Road," "Harrison's Road," "Road to Louisville," "Vincennes Trace," "Buffalo Trail," etc. William Rector was surveyor-general of Illinois, Missouri and Arkansas, from 1814 to 1824.

75

[149] American State Papers, Class II, Indian Affairs, pp. 689-690.

[150] Miscellaneous Record I, pp. 37-39; *Early Travels in Indiana,* pp. 17, 18, 19, 359-365; Note 2 in Indiana Historical Society's Publications, Vol. 3, p. 97, Vol. 2, pp. 16 and 464, Vol. 4, p. 190, Vol. 5, pp. 47-54; "The Public Domain," Vol. 19, p. 171.

SURVEY OF THE GROUSELAND TREATY LINE, IN 1806.

In July and August, 1806, Arthur Henri, a government surveyor, ran the Grouseland treaty line from the Freeman corner, near Orleans, to near Brookville. He began at the Freeman corner and ran a random line north 65° east, intending to strike the Fort Recovery Indian treaty boundary line (the gore line) 50 miles from the mouth of the Kentucky river. He struck 15 miles and 77 chains too far south. Then he began at a point 50 miles north of the mouth of the Kentucky river, and ran back to the Freeman corner, which he missed by running south. He then corrected his line back. The distance was 89 miles and 45.5 chains. The ten o'clock line intersects this line at a point 30 miles from the Freeman corner.

SURVEY OF THE "TEN O'CLOCK LINE," THE NORTHEAST LINE OF THE HARRISON PURCHASE.

This treaty line crosses the mouth of Raccoon creek, in Vermillion county, passes through Gosport, in Owen county, and ends on the Grouseland treaty line in Jackson county, at a point on the said line 30 miles from Orleans; that is, 30 miles from the northeast Freeman corner. The county line between Ripley and Decatur counties is the course of the Grouseland treaty line. It is the Grouseland treaty line while also the county line. The survey of the ten o'clock line was made by John McDonald, deputy surveyor for the government.[151] Many interesting things are mentioned in the rec-

151 *Early Travels in Indiana,* pp. 75, 86, 88, 99, 170, 199, 231, 242, 491; Miscellaneous Record I, p. 119; Indiana Historical Society's Publications, Vol. 1, p. 158; Vol. 4, map, p. 176, Vol. 3, p. 159; (Not of Dubois County); Vol. 5, pp. 55 and 112, Vol. 2, p. 34, Vol. 6, p. 303, Vol. 6, p. 312;

ords of this survey. Part of the "Harrison Purchase" was in Illinois. At 68.85 chains north 53° 45′ west of the mouth of Raccoon creek, on the north line of the "Harrison Purchase," in Vermillion county, not far from Hillsdale, the records show a mound about 9 chains in circumference, and 1 chain in elevation.[152] About 2 miles east of Dana the record shows an Indian trace. The corner in Illinois was reached January 11, 1811, and is 15.16 miles from Raccoon creek.[153]

On the "Market Highway" (also known as the "Jackson Highway" and "French Lick Route"), between Seymour and Brownstown, and near a cemetery, is a marker erected to guide one to where the "Ten O'Clock Line" intersects the Grouseland treaty line, before mentioned. Thus the termini of this line are brought to view.

The so-called "Ten O'clock Line" is on the northeast side of the "Harrison Purchase," or the southwest side of the "New Purchase." [154] It begins where Raccoon creek enters the Wabash river in Parke county, and runs south 53° 45′ east about 95 miles to a point near Brownstown, where it intersects the Grouseland treaty line. The surveyor's record shows that 13 miles and 30.25 chains from the mouth of Raccoon creek, an Indian trail, leading southwest, crossed the line.[155] This is near Bridgeton, Indiana. At 48 miles and 4.65 chains from Raccoon creek an Indian trail was crossed. This trail passed through Gosport, and probably led to the spring in Gosport. At 48 miles and 43.40 chains the line struck White river, at Gosport, where the river ran south

[152] Miscellaneous Record I, p. 115.

[153] Miscellaneous Record I, pp. 115-119; The "Western Gazetteer" (1817), p. 64.

[154] *Early Travels in Indiana*, pp. 80, 86, 98, 99 and 231; Indiana Historical Society's Publications, Vol. 4, p. 304, Vol. 6, p. 326.

[155] Miscellaneous Record I, p. 73.

10° west, (which is almost south). At 3.40 chains from the right-hand bank of the river there used to be a cherry tree and a sugar tree.[156] At 71 miles and 21 chains from Raccoon creek another Indian trail crossed the line. This was 10 miles east of Bloomington.[157] Just before the line hit the Grouseland treaty line another Indian trail was noted.[158] The old survey maps show a high bluff and a stone quarry along the bank of White river, and near the center of section 32, now Monon station.[159]

The "Ten O'clock Line" was run by John McDonald, of Vincennes, a government treaty surveyor. In 1816 some section lines south of it were run by A. Henri and William Harris. In 1819, some north of it were surveyed by Thomas Brown, John Collett, and others. Gosport happens to be an equal distance from the two Indian ends of the line.[160]

The treaty defining this "Ten O'clock Line" was made at Fort Wayne, September 30, 1809, and it was signed by William Henry Harrison, on the part of the United States. This treaty was the outcome of a series of negotiations by which the United States acquired the title to about 2,900,000 acres, the greater part of which lay above the old Vincennes tract ceded by the Indians in 1803, and above the Grouseland treaty, which came later. The treaty covered all the land in Indiana from Brownstown to Orleans, thence to Merom, from Merom to Raccoon creek, and thence by this "Ten O'clock Line" to Brownstown.

By the year 1809, the total quantity of land ceded to the

156 Miscellaneous Record I, p. 90.
157 Miscellaneous Record I, p. 101.
158 Miscellaneous Record I, p. 115.
159 Plat Book 2, p. 17, State Auditor's Office.
160 *Early Travels in Indiana*, pp. 75 and 87; Indiana Historical Society's Publications, Vol. 5, pp. 56-112.

United States under treaties which were concluded between Governor Harrison and various Indian tribes, amounted to almost 30,000,000 acres.

The consummation of this treaty was one of the principal and immediate causes which led up to the great controversy with Tecumseh, and the stirring events that follow, including the battle of Tippecanoe; and it is but a flight of the imagination to conclude that the "Ten O'clock Line" made William Henry Harrison president of the United States.[161]

There is a tradition to the effect that the Indians were very troublesome while the line was being surveyed. Tradition says they did not trust the compass, and preferred the shadow made by the sun and a staff at ten o'clock in the morning, because the white man could not manipulate the sun as he could a compass. Therefore, the common expression, the "Ten O'clock Line." This is a pretty story, to say the least. At the time Indiana became a state, in 1816, this line was the north line of Indiana, under white government. The centennial we celebrated in 1916 really belonged to those south of the line. What is now Gosport was the very edge of the line, and on the Indian frontier.

The Indians began to see themselves losing the land, and the tribes in the central and northern parts of Indiana began to see white men to the south of them, where once roamed warriors of their own color. The government surveyors who immediately entered the land after the treaties were signed, began to divide the forests into sections, ready for the land-officers and settlers. Two hundred fifty thousand forest trees bearing the marks of the surveyors, tokens of advancing civilization, told the Indians, in a manner not to be misunder-

79

[161] *Early Travels in Indiana,* p. 32; See decorations Fowler Hotel, LaFayette.

stood, that the days of the forest were numbered, and that their possessions were passing away.[162]

Tecumseh was an Indian statesman, in addition to being a warrior. He contended that the Indians held their land in common, and that no one tribe or family could properly convey a part of the Indian territory to the whites. He endeavored to have the Indians unite and to consider their lands as the common property of the whole. He accused General Harrison of taking tribes aside and advising them not to unite or enter into Tecumseh's confederacy. The sale of the land south of our "Ten O'clock Line" brought forth a remonstrance from Tecumseh, and in time, the dissatisfaction among the Indian warriors caused by the treaty led to the battle of Tippecanoe, in 1811.

80

STATE LINE SURVEYS.

SURVEY OF THE NORTH PART OF THE OHIO AND INDIANA STATE LINE.

The east line of Indiana, north of the Greenville treaty line, was surveyed by William Harris, in 1817, and E. P. Kendricks in 1827;[163] the last ten miles being surveyed by E. P. Kendricks. These ten miles had been taken from Michigan and added to Indiana. The northeast corner of Indiana, and the northwest corner of Ohio are not identical. In 1827, when the northeast corner of Indiana was established by Surveyor Kendricks, he made a record of 8 witness trees, so as

---

[162] Indiana Historical Society's Publications, Vol. 3, pp. 101 and 102, Vol. 6, p. 308.

[163] Miscellaneous Record I, p. 198.

to securely preserve its location.[164] (In 1817, William Harris ran a line due east of the south end of Lake Michigan, a distance of 40 miles or more, the 44th mile post being 9.83 chains east of the second principal meridian. At 38 miles east of Lake Michigan, Harris located an Indian village. This was about 8 miles east of Laporte, and 2 miles north of Fish Lake.)

A substantial cylindrical monument marks the Ohio and Indiana state line, just north of the Baltimore & Ohio railroad, and on the Cincinnati and Lawrenceburg pike. The line is 7° 45′ longitude west from the city of Washington,[165] which is generally placed at 77° 1′ 34″ west of Greenwich. The General Land Office places the Indiana-Ohio line at 84° 48′ 10″ west of Greenwich, England. It is 182 miles, 61 chains and 44 links from the northeast corner of Indiana to the Miami and Ohio rivers.

81

SURVEY OF THE INDIANA AND ILLINOIS STATE LINE.

This line starts at a point on the northwest or right-hand bank of the Wabash river, 46 miles *due north of Vincennes,* from which point a sycamore 38 inches in diameter bears north 71° west, 20 links distant, and a second sycamore 30

[164] Miscellaneous Record I, p. 201; Indians often referred to "line trees," or "witness trees" as "trees of peace,"—Indiana and Indianans, Vol. I, p. 58.

[165] Indiana Historical Society's Publications, Vol. 3, pp. 65, 67, 114-116; Dillon's *History of Indiana*, p. 1; Lippincott's *New Gazetteer*, p. 1959; Miscellaneous Record I, pp. 1 and 208; *Early Travels in Indiana*, pp. 136, 198, 216, 244, 269, 443, 497 and 523; *The Western Gazetteer*, Brown's, p. 37; *"Footprints of the Pioneers,"* by Venable, p. 27; Read "The Articles of Compact';; "Constitution Making in Indiana," Vol. I, 51 and 74; (For boundaries of Indiana, see Constitution of Indiana, Sec. I, Art. 14).

inches bears north 84° east, 39 links distant.[166] By June 9,
1821, the surveyors had reached the fifteenth mile (near
Sanford, Indiana,) going north at a variation of 6° 25'.[167]
The twenty-seventh mile was reached on June 10th.
At 76 miles and 65 chains the line crossed the south line
of the Saint Mary's purchase.[168] At 122 miles and 38
chains a river was reached, and on the record is noted:
"Illinois river or Kankakee river, so called here." On Monday, July 2, 1821, Lake Michigan was reached at 159 miles
and 44 chains, and its waters at 159 miles and 46 chains.
John McDonald was the Deputy United States Surveyor.
This point was 11 miles, 4 chains and 46 links west, and 6
miles, 15 chains and 86 links north of the lake's southern extremity.[169] In February and March, 1834, the line was re-
traced from the 118th mile post north, by S. Sibley, Deputy
Surveyor. He rebuilt many of Surveyor McDonald's old
mounds. A large post was set in the sand bank on the bor-
der of Lake Michigan.[170] Sylvester Sibley, Deputy Surveyor, re-surveyed the Indiana and Illinois state line in pur-
suance to instructions from M. F. Williams, Surveyor General of the United States, under date of July 1, 1833. John
Hodgson and Peter S. Galloway were the chainmen, and William Howard was the marker. The line is 11° 1' of longitude west of the city of Washington.[171] The General Land

82

166 Miscellaneous Record I, p. 121; *Early Travels in Indiana,* p. 136.

167 Miscellaneous Record I, p. 123; Indiana Historical Society's Publications, Vol. 3, p. 67, Vol. 4, pp. 201 and 223.

168 Miscellaneous Record I, p. 133.

169 Miscellaneous Record I, p. 143; *Early Travels in Indiana,* p. 86.

170 Miscellaneous Record I, pp. 1 and 152.

171 Miscellaneous Record I, p. 152; *Early Travels in Indiana,* pp. 198,
216, 244, 269, 443, 497, 523; Dillon's *History of Indiana,* p. 1; "Constitution Making in Indiana," Vol. 1, pp. 41, 51 and 74; Constitution of
Indiana, Sec. 1, Art. 14.

Office places it at 87° 31' 50" west of Greenwich, England.
A government marker on the bank of the Wabash at Vincennes places its own longitude at 87° 32' 27.79" west of
Greenwich.   It also records its own latitude at 38° 48'
37.71" The bench mark on the court house shows the elevation to be 429.928.   Vincennes was the *governing point*
for the Illinois and Indiana state line.

SURVEY OF THE MICHIGAN AND INDIANA STATE LINE.

In 1827, E. P. Kendricks surveyed the northern boundary
of Indiana.   On October 8th, he commenced at the southern extremity of Lake Michigan, at a corner that had been
established by Surveyor Harris, in 1817.   The cedar post[172]
placed by Surveyor Harris was entirely covered by sand, but
Surveyor Kendricks found it by reason of having two aspen
trees as pointers.   The Michigan and Indiana line starts east
10 miles north of the south end of Lake Michigan.[173]   He
found the place by latitudes and departures.   The Indiana
and Michigan state line was marked on the east shore of
Lake Michigan, by a pine tree 10 inches in diameter.   The
north side was marked "M. L." (Michigan Line) ; the south
side, "I. L." (Indiana Line.)   He used 6° 10' as his variation.   He reached the second principal meridian at 18
miles and 43.17 chains.

At 38 miles and 22 chains he recorded a road from Fort
Wayne to Chicago.   (This is about the northwest corner
of Elkhart county.)   At 77 miles and 37 chains he recorded

83

[172] Indiana Historical Society's Publications, Vol. 4, pp. 201 and 223,
Vol. 3, pp. 65, 114 and 116; Miscellaneous Record I, p. 203.
[173] Miscellaneous Record I, p. 155; *Early Travels in Indiana*, p. 136.

a trail from Fort Wayne to Nottawsepe.[174]   (This was 6 miles west of the northeast corner of LaGrange county.) The north line was full of tamarisk marshes and swamps.   At 93 miles and 7 chains a trail ran north and south.   At 93 miles and 25.50 chains a trail crossed from Coldwater to Fort Wayne.[175]   These were just north of Fremont, Indiana, and probably led to James Lake, or smaller lakes near by.) At 94 miles and 60 chains a trail ran north and south.[176] The northeast corner of Indiana is 104 miles and 49.55 chains east of Lake Michigan.   North latitude 41° 50', also recorded 42° 10', and 41° 43', etc.   The General Land Office places it at 41° 45' 35" north latitude.[177]

84

INDIAN AND OTHER RESERVATIONS.

OLD FRENCH SURVEYS.

These tracts of land are in the main, to be found only in the "Vincennes Tract," generally only in Knox county. To satisfy the claims of the old French settlers, the United States directed to be set apart all the lands bounded on the west by the Wabash river; on the south by White river; on the east by the west branch of White river, and on the north by the Freeman line. Four hundred acres was the usual assign-

[174] Miscellaneous Record I, p. 181.
[175] Miscellaneous Record I, p. 185.
[176] Miscellaneous Record I, p. 186.
[177] Miscellaneous Record I, pp. 1 and 189; *Early Travels in Indiana,* pp. 136, 198, 216, 244, 269, 443, 497 and 523; Dillon's *History of Indiana,* p. 1; "Constitution Making in Indiana," Vol. 1, pp. 41, 43, 47, 51 and 74; (For boundaries of Indiana, read Sec. 1, Art. 14, Constitution of Indiana).

ment to each person entitled to a donation. A French system was used. The tracts are very narrow and long, and run at right angles to rivers. The government surveyors in charge of the rectangular system, measured up to these lines and there closed their surveys. Very artistic maps were made of these surveys. In fact the most artistic maps in the state house are those hand-made maps in the plat books of the early government surveys in southern Indiana.[178] These French surveys were due to the fact that the United States confirmed the French in their possessions.

SURVEY OF THE MIAMI NATIONAL RESERVE, 1838-1839.

This reserve was surveyed in 1838 and 1839, under adverse circumstances. The survey began below the mouth of the Salamania river, and meandered down the "southerly" bank of the Wabash river. At 56 chains above the mouth of the Mississinewa river (near Peru), the Indian town of Mississinewa was located. At the mouth of the Mississinewa river the surveyors set a post 9 inches in diameter, with a "May pole" marked with 18 notches, and two sycamore trees as witnesses. The surveyor entered the following in his record: "Here the Indians held another council on the 6th of the month (November, 1819) which was much against me. My provisions were much wasted here, as we had to accompany their chiefs to the town, where the Indians made free with my bread. On the seventh they added another chief to my party, which I had to support with bread and meat."[179]

85

---

[178] Brown's *"Western Gazetteer,"* pp. 66 and 67; *Early Travels in Indiana,* pp. 76, 77, 101, 160, 161, 230, 461; Plat Book V, p. 157, etc.; Indiana Historical Society's Publications, Vol. 2, pp. 425-434.

[179] Miscellaneous Record I, p. 215.

At the mouth of Eel river the surveyors set a wild cherry post 9 inches in diameter. The date "1819" was marked on top. Near by a beech tree was marked "34½ M.", being the number of miles from the mouth of Salamonie river. It was also marked "M. K. T." There were also a sugar tree and a white oak for markers. This was on November 9, 1819. At this place the surveying party was detained by the Indians until November 11, 1819. This was the west side of the reserve, and about 5 miles east of the second principal meridian. The site is now recognized as Logansport.[180] From here the line ran south 34 miles and 43.20 chains. Eleven miles south of Logansport, near Deer creek, the Indians again became dissatisfied. At 17 miles and 30 chains the surveyor crossed a small river 200 links wide, which he named St. John's. At 28½ miles south of Logansport he crossed a road leading to an Indian village. This was about 7 miles northeast of Frankfort.

In writing of the southwest corner of the reserve, which is near Kirklin, Indiana, the surveyor noted: "We set the southwest corner of the reserve; a wild cherry post 9 inches in diameter, with the date of the year '1819' cut on top." On a beech he cut "S. W. cor. 34½ m. reserve, F. M. N.", and the date "1819." An ash was also recorded as a witness tree. On another beech, within the reserve, he cut "N. S. M. K. T. 1819, 34½ M." From here he started east, and when he had gone 1 mile the Indians became dissatisfied.[181] He ran north 79° 51' East, 34 miles and 43.20 chains, passing south of Tipton, and established the southeast corner of the Miami National Reserve. (In time this reserve was ceded to the United States by treaties under date of October 23, 1834, November 6, 1838, and November 28, 1840.)

180 *Early Travels in Indiana*, p. 13.
181 Miscellaneous Record I, p. 220.

86

At the southeast corner of the reserve he set a white oak post 10 inches in diameter, and 5 feet high. The top of it was marked "1819." A beech tree was marked "S. E. cor. of 34½ M. R. S. I. A. 1819;" another beech tree was marked "M. R. 34½ M. M. K. T. 1819." A white oak and a hickory stood near by. This corner is near Alexandria and Rigdon. The survey then went north to the mouth of the Salamonia river at Lagro. When the surveyor had reached 14 miles and 36.50 chains, which was west of Marion, and about 8 miles south of LaFontaine, he made this record in his field notes: "Here the Indians, in an imperious manner told me I was going wrong, and said I should go no farther that way, saying that I was going to go to their town and if I would not go 10 miles east of the town they would not let me go on. I saw by their looks and the way they behaved that I was unsafe, so I stopped. They would scarcely permit me to make a mark and appeared displeased. We left the line and started for Fort Recovery (Ohio) where we arrived on the 29th of the month. (November 29, 1819.)

"J. S. ALLEN, *D. S.*"

The next paragraph begins: "March 18, 1820. Began where the Indians stopped me on the 25th of November, 1819." The record shows that he completed the survey on March 20, 1820. He began November 3, 1818.[182]

In November, 1838, the Miami Indians sold a tract of land along the northeast line of the reserve, and the survey was made May 9th, 10th and 11th, 1839, by A. St. C. Vance,[183] Deputy Surveyor. In this survey a record is made of a road leading from Deer creek to Peru. The line ran through an

---

[182] Miscellaneous Record I, p. 225.
[183] Miscellaneous Record I, pp. 226-231.

Indian village on Pipe creek, containing about 10 houses,[184] and crossed many Indian trails or paths. This Indian treaty line was about 20 miles long and ran east and west not far from LaFontaine, which is near the southeast corner.

THORNTOWN RESERVE.

In the survey of the "Thorntown Reserve," in 1822, a record is made of an Indian trace leading from Fort Wayne to Fort Harrison. Near by was a cluster of Indian wigwams. This trace could be easily re-located from the survey records which are exceptionally complete. The surveyor was Thomas Brown.[185]

CHIEF RICHARDVILLE'S RESERVE.

88

In October, 1819, Surveyor Joseph A. Allen laid out a reservation for Chief Richardville, opposite the mouth of "Little River." It contained two sections."[186]

RACCOON VILLAGE RESERVE.

In September, 1827, Surveyor Chauncey Carter surveyed the Raccoon Village Reserve, on A'boite river. This survey located several Indian roads that led to Fort Wayne.[187] During this same month Surveyor Carter also ran the boundary line from Tippecanoe river to Eel river.

[184] Miscellaneous Record I, p. 228; Indiana Historical Society's Publications, Vol. 1, p. 152.

[185] Miscellaneous Record I, p. 265; Indiana Historical Society's Publications, Vol. 6, p. 314; Brown's *"Western Gazetteer,"* p. 72.

[186] Miscellaneous Record I, pp. 271 and 272.

[187] Miscellaneous Record I, p. 276.

SEEK'S VILLAGE AND METEA'S VILLAGE.

Seek's village was on the southeast side of Eel river, and in November, 1827, a line was run from it to Metea's village, by Chauncey Carter.[188] In the plat of this survey many willow swamps and Indian trails are noted. Metea's village was on the banks of Cedar creek, near its junction with St. Joseph's river.[189] There was a reserve of 14 sections at Seek's village.

MISSISSINEWA RESERVE.

In the survey of a reserve five miles wide opposite the mouth of Mississinewa river, an Indian village is noted. The survey was made in July, 1827. Many islands are noted in the streams. Chauncey Carter made the survey, and made a very specific record of "line trees," etc.[190]

89

WYANDOT VILLAGE RESERVE.

The Wyandot village reserve of five sections was surveyed for Jean B. Richardville, Long Hair, and others, and began at a spring in the center of the village. The reserve was on Wild Cat creek. The survey was made in September, 1823, by P. F. Kellogg. He also made a division for the Burnetts of their six sections,[191] located below the mouth of the Tippecanoe river. Their names were Abraham, Isaac, James and Rebecca.

188 Miscellaneous Record I, pp. 291, 295 and 300.
189 Miscellaneous Record I, p. 295.
190 Miscellaneous Record I, p. 313.
191 Miscellaneous Record I, p. 319.

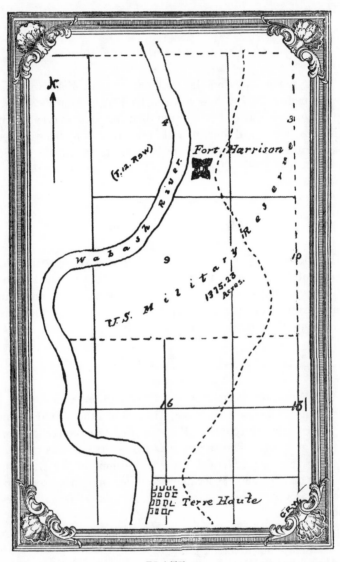

90

PLATE 11.

The above is a tracing of the official government hand-made map
with the technical figures of the surveyor omitted. The tracing shows
only that part of the reservation nearest the fort.

SUGAR CREEK RESERVE.

The Sugar creek reserve was on the west bank of the Wabash river and north of the mouth of Raccoon creek. It included an Indian village and joined the north line of the Harrison Purchase for the first seven miles easterly from the mouth of Raccoon creek, commonly known as the "Ten O'clock Line." The survey was made by William Harris.[192]

TECHNICAL LOCATION OF FORT HARRISON.

Fort Harrison was located by the government surveyors in section 4 near Terre Haute. The old Plat Book number 2, pages 84 and 85 has a very good drawing indicating the location of the fort. The military reservation around it contained 1,375.23 acres. Another military reservation of 487 acres was located across the river and to the north.[193]

91

TYPICAL ROAD AND SWAMP SURVEYS.

THE MICHIGAN ROAD SURVEYS.

In 1828, a survey of the Michigan road 100 feet wide, began where Trail creek emptied into Lake Michigan. It came to Indi-

[192] Miscellaneous Record I, p. 329.

[193] Indiana Historical Society's Publications, Volume 1, p. 178; Volume 2, p. 131; Volume 3, p. 55 and 280; Map p. 176, Volume 4; Volume 6, pp. 305, 306 and 310; Dillon's *History of Indiana*, pp. 462, 489 and 578; *Early Travels in Indiana*, pp. 68, 69, 79, 87, 88, 89, 96, 131, 135, 145, 161, 211, 232, 233 and 444; Brown's *Western Gazetteer*, (1817), pp. 47 and 48. pp. 68, 69.

anapolis "by the south bend of the St. Joseph river and Eel river" [Logansport] and ended in front of "the governor's house in the town of Indianapolis." The commissioners on this part were John I. Neely, Chester Elliott and John McDonald. Where South Bend now stands was the "American Fur Company's Establishment." The map of this part of the road is well drawn, and contains a desperate attempt to sketch the governor's house, at the end of the map. In the field notes, about the thirty-eighth mile from Lake Michigan are these words: "At this [point] is a beautiful cite [site] for a town."[194] South Bend is the answer. The surveyor's record or entry bears date of November 3 and 4, 1828. John McDonald and John K. Graham were the surveyors.

The field notes of the south half of the road show that the survey began at Madison, on Monday, May 17, 1830, and that a state road was to be laid out from Madison, through Indianapolis, to Lake Michigan. The act creating this southern commission was approved January 30, 1830. William Polk, Abraham McClellan and Samuel Hanna were the commissioners. Thomas Reaugh was the surveyor. A good map accompanies the survey records. The road was surveyed by "calls," i. e. courses and distances. The two parts of the Michigan road met at Indianapolis. A monument marks the point where the Madison division entered Washington street.[195]

[194] *Early Travels in Indiana,* p. 144; Indiana Historical Society's Publications, Volume 2, pp. 196 and 438; Brown's *Western Gazetteer,* (1817) pp. 45-47.

[195] Records on file with the State Auditor; Indiana Historical Society's Publications, Volume 5, pp. 55-60—a good article; see Map p.40, Volume 5, also p. 112; Dillon's *History of Indiana,* p. 571.

TRAILS AND SURVEYS

KIBBEY'S ROAD.

In Dearborn county there is an old road known as "Kibbey's Road." It is marked on the records by surveyors. It entered Dearborn county at the Greenville treaty line near Holman and went east, south of Manchester. Another old trail ran east and west, north of Aurora, Cochran, and south of Chesterville.[196] The Kibbey road ran from Cincinnati to Vincennes.

SURVEYING THE SWAMPS OF THE KANKAKEE RIVER, ETC.

The survey of northwestern Indiana was a source of much hard work on the part of the "swamp Moses." The records left by the surveyors of that part of Indiana were so full of lamentations that they would have put Jeremiah to shame, yet so faithful and patient were the surveyors that Job would have found his equal. Let us hope their rewards were in proportion.

In commenting upon township 33 north, range 6 west, about Aylesworth, in Porter county, Surveyor Uriah Biggs, in his report of January 5, 1835, says: "This township is generally unsusceptible of cultivation. A small portion of the north part only, can be cultivated. The Kankakee river is rather a sluggish stream, its banks very low and lined on each side with a heavy growth of timber, mostly ash, some elm, maple, oak and birch, which grow very tall, and is undergrown with swamp alder and wild rose, etc., making an interminable forest which is covered with water during the sea-

[196] Plat Book 1, pp. 39-45; Indiana Historical Society's Publications, Volume 2, p. 107; Volume I, pp. 256, 259, 260, 279, 292, 294, 340, 341 and 347.

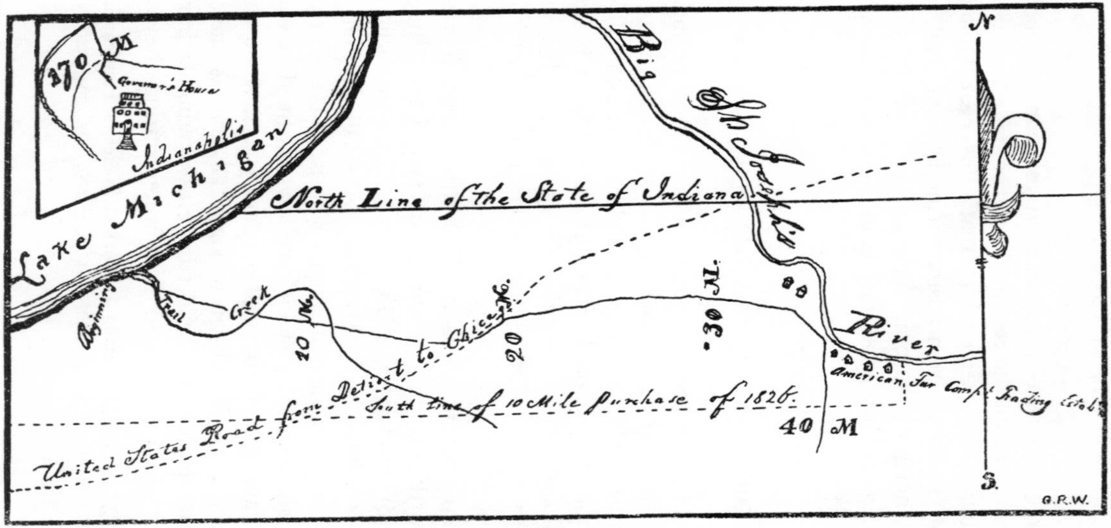

94

PLATE 12.

(Memo.—The above was sketched from the original map. The inset shows the end of the survey at Indianapolis. Michigan City, at the mouth of Trail creek, marks the beginning. The old American Fur Company Post is now South Bend.—G. R. W.)

son. The soil in this forest or swamp is loose yellow sand which renders it almost impracticable to approach the river, only when the swamp is frozen. In the marshes on the north part of the township there are large beds of rich iron ore."[197] Practically all surveyors reported iron ore in these swamps in northwest Indiana.

In 1835, in speaking of the Yellow river, Jeremiah Smith, the surveyor of township 33 north, range 3 west, says: "The line could not be seen, as it lay principally in the expanded water of Yellow river, which is here mingling with and assuming the garb of its mother, Kankakee."[198] The same surveyor laid out township 34, and in his record says: "There is but little room left for general remarks in this township. There is such an endless sameness of marsh, interspersed with a few groves of timber that there is nothing upon which to digress from the monotony of lamentation. There seems to be every indication of iron ore in this township, also, but I am not mineralogist sufficient to say positively that there is any, or in what abundance it exists."[199] The surveyors of township 36 north, range 5 west, and of township 31 north of range 6 west, also reported iron ore.[200] There was, no doubt, a "needle disturbance" that led to the report of iron ore. Just what caused this disturbance is not known.

Jeremiah Smith, in his report on township 33 north, range 1 west, which is known as Washington township, in Starke county, says: "The upland rolling parts of this township have a loose white sandy soil, in some places so loose that a person will sink an inch or two in walking over it. But little vegetation or undergrowth or shrubbery here. On the parts

95

[197] Record 22, *North and West*, p. 430.
[198] Record 20, *North and West*, p. 437.
[199] Record 20, *North and West*, p. 477.
[200] Record 22, *North and West*, pp. 220 and 360.

lower or more level the soil though still sandy assumes a more yellowish and in some places very near a black clay. The prairies are either dry, by which I mean such as can be cultivated, or they are wet, or they are wet and marshy. The soil of the prairie is generally black, but the dry spots are so few and far between that tilling is out of the question, yet a good part of them are excellent for grazing. South of Yellow river in sections 19, 20 and 29 is as rich a pasturage as is to be found anywhere. The grass is thickly set and looks like an oat-field just before it heads. In it were a few Indian ponies keeping fat and wallowing in nature's choicest luxuries. Some of the prairies are too marshy for grazing, and what use they can be put to, I can't tell. The river is very crooked and full of timber. Its bottoms on its right bank are from one-fourth to three-fourths of a mile wide, which is very thickly set with a tall heavy growth of timber in which is to be found nearly all the varieties of the continent. The soil is black and rich and would be valuable were it not that it overflows, has bayous through it, or stink-holes filled with stagnant water, or a black alder and rose-brier pond, or marsh. Some or all of these things are so perpetually occurring as to render the land of little or no value, only for the timber. South of the river or on its left bank is prairie, irregular in its width and generally wet. Sometimes the timber gets over onto the south side, or rather the river runs northward into the timber, but it soon returns. Eagle creek runs through a marshy prairie, the whole way, though it sometimes is very narrow and always wet." [201]

On April 22, 1834, this same surveyor, Jeremiah Smith, in commenting on township 34, range 1 west, makes this record: "The general appearance of this township [Oregon, in Starke

[201] Record IX, pp. 225, 226 and 227; Brown's *Western Gazetteer*, 1817, pp. 45-46, 78.

county] is rather uninviting to the capitalist and land speculator, but to the poor man and him who wishes to act the 'squatter' it holds out some inducements. The soil is generally sandy, on the rolling parts loose and white with but little soil or vegetation; on the lower and more level parts the land is more compact and of a darker color and generally pretty good sod or coat of roots, matted or near the surface. In the wet prairies the sods are from 6 to 18 inches in height and about the same dimensions as to length and breadth. Their distances asunder include every change of space from zero or 0 to 12 inches and of all the places ever a poor wight had to walk over with 'heads up' and 'eyes front' they are the worst. The marshes or marsh prairies are more smooth to walk over, but not a bit more pleasant to walk over than the prairies, for though we have not the stubby sods to be stumbling over continually we have water and a marshy substance to wade through and the whole placed upon a yielding elastic sod; all of which combined makes the labour of traversing them almost worthy to be laid along side and considered a parallel with the labour in the retreat of Henophen with his ten thousand Greeks."

"On sections 10 and 15 and a part of section 16 is some pretty good land which would pay a man for cultivation. The balance of the town is either too wet to cultivate or so poor as not to justify cultivation, but a great part of it is very good for grazing, and that is why I think squatters may be induced to come here, as they need not be in fear of being bought out. On the northeast shore of Woodworth's Lake is a pretty eminence to build on in view of the lake but it is ruined by having a miserable tamarisk swamp right ferninst (opposite) its back."[202]

[202] Record IX, *North and West*, pp. 262 and 263.

Surveyor Smiths' parents evidently knew why they called him "Jeremiah"—perhaps they anticipated his ability at lamentations.

On June 21, 1834, Surveyor William Clark, in closing his record of his survey of township 36 north, range 1 west, near Fish Lake, in Laporte county, says: "The Kankakee river and its branches present the appearance of ponds or lakes rather than running streams, and are inaccessible in almost every place. There are many places near the shores where the weight of a man will shake the marshes for acres together." [203]

Samuel Goodnow, surveyor of township 31 north, range 9 west, at Lake Village, in Newton county, on March 3, 1835, makes this entry: "A great portion of this township is not prairie, or in other words entirely a marsh. There is a small portion of timber growing along the margin of the Kankakee river; the whole township bears the aspect of that of the surrounding country, alike interspersed with sand ridges which are dry, and denotes a country destitute of any inducement to invite the emigrant to locate there. The marshes are principally covered with alder and wild rice. The timber upon the sand ridge before mentioned is black and white oak, and some under bush; that along the river, birch, maple, swamp ash and some willow. In many places it is difficult to tell where the bed of the Kankakee river is placed. Such is the unfavorable aspect of the country that I cannot in justice give a more flattering character and keep within bounds of all matters pertaining to facts." [204]

And thus run the records along the Kankakee almost all its course through Indiana. Early travelers called that part of Indiana the "champaign country."

[203] Record IX, *North and West*, p. 341.
[204] Record 24, *North and West*, p. 185; Brown's *Western Gazetteer*, 1817, p. 43.

98

INTERESTING DISCOVERIES AND INCIDENTS RECORDED BY THE SURVEYORS.

The surveyors, following their instructions, not only recorded important physical features of the country surveyed, but occasionally recorded some unusual and important incident occuring while making their surveys. A few of their discoveries and incidents are deemed of sufficient importance to be here noted.

GOVERNMENT SURVEYORS LOCATE FRENCH LICK AND WEST BADEN SPRINGS.

On November 22-24, 1804, Edward W. Tupper and Augustus Stone, Deputy Government Surveyors, were surveying in township 1, north range 2 west, near French Lick. Their field notes contain this memorandum:

"In section 3, 5 chains and 60 links due south from 49 chains and 50 links, on last mile (S. E. cor. Sec. 34) is a salt spring breaking out at the foot of a hill near the surface of the ground. The quality of the water I could not ascertain, but the quantity appeared to me to be sufficient to form a sheet of water two feet wide and one inch deep. About 4 chains southeast of this spring is another *salt* spring affording more than double the quantity of water which appeared at the first spring, [French Lick.] Those two springs uniting with a fresh water spring which breaks out between the two continue along near the surface of the ground, and form a brook or creek of from 12 to 20 feet in width, in the bottom of which at a number of places may be seen other *salt* springs boiling up through the fresh water. And though the several fresh and salt springs uniting form a stream 6 or 8 inches deep and of at least 16 feet in width; yet some distance below where the springs appear the whole creek appears strongly impregnated with salt. Other springs make their appearance, when the waters are low in the branch of what I call *Salt Lick Creek* as it runs through the next mile square north, or in section 34, in township 2 north, range 2 west. [West Baden.] I am well convinced any quantity of salt water might be obtained by digging in case the springs are found weaker than the quantity of salt water in general. It will be necessary to *reserve* the section 34 in township 2 north range, 2 west, as the appearance for salt water by digging is equally as good on that side of the line as in section 3, township 1 north, range 2 west, south of that mile-square."[205]

The surveyors did not give the springs their names. French Lick and West Baden are indicated on the survey plats of 1804, as "Salt Springs, on Salt Creek," and running down the creek a distance of two miles.[206]

FOOTE'S POND SURVEY, RATTLE SNAKE DEN.

Foote's Grave Pond is in Gibson county, in sections 15, 16, 21 and 22, township 3, south range 13 west. Near the west bank is an ancient mound 30 feet high.[207] The pond was finally surveyed in 1844, by Nath. L. Squibb. In his field notes he records finding "a den where 300 rattle-snakes are said to have been killed in one day."[208] He also seems to

---

205 Brown's *Western Gazetteer,* 1817, pp. 49, 64 and 65 and 80; *Early Travels in Indiana,* pp. 60, 61 and 521; Volume 2, *North and West,* pp. 81 and 82.

206 Plat Book V, pp. 138 and 139; *Early Travels in Indiana,* pp. 60, 61, 278 and 521; *Sylvia Scarlet,* by Compton Mackenzie.

207 Plat Book V, p. 88.

208 Record 10, West, p. 185; *Early Travels in Indiana,* p. 170.

have had great difficulty in his survey, for he closes his entry thus: "Spent one-half day searching No. 2 [a corner] and found none. Could get no corners better than to run the lines from Foote's pond and from the assurance of all the hunters we found that there was nothing but a brushy slue; [slough] there, we left it."

In 1806, William Rector made some of the original field notes of township 3,[209] and also made part of the survey. It is quite likely that Foote's field notes were lost with him. The pond is about 20 chains across and almost 1 mile long.[210] The official field notes, as now known, do not record the accident that cost Foote's life.[211] The story of the accident is as follows: Ziba Foote, then not twenty-one, lost his life April 30, 1806, in the pond which bears his name, in this manner:

101

He was conducting a government survey about the pond, and attempted to pass through the pond with his compass and Jacob-staff fastened to his belt. In this condition he had gone but a short distance when he got over his depth, and being encumbered by his compass and staff, sank to rise no more. Two hours afterward his body was recovered. His remains were placed in a bark coffin and buried late that evening on a small hill near the pond. He was born in Newtown, Connecticut, July 4, 1785, graduated at Yale with great honor, at the age of twenty. He was surveying under the direction of William Rector, deputy surveyor to Surveyor General Mansfield, of Cincinnati, when he lost his life. Many years after the accident his remains were removed to Bedford, Indiana, by his brother, Dr. W. Foote, and placed

---

[209] Record 10, p. 83.

[210] Plat Book V, p. 89.

[211] *Early Travels in Indiana,* p. 170; Indiana Historical Society's Publications, Volume 2, pp. 359-365.

in a native stone sepulcher near Bedford. The complete story forms an interesting chapter of early Indiana history.[212]

N. HARLAN'S FERRY, IN PIKE COUNTY.

Township 1 north, range 9 west, was surveyed by H. Bradley, D. Sullivan and R. Buntin in 1805 and 1807. In their surveys they meandered both banks of White river. Harlan's Ferry touched the south, or left-hand bank of White river at 41 chains up the river from the south line of section 1, and the right-hand bank of the river at 22.50 chains down the river from the east line of said section 1. This makes a very exact description of the route of the ferry boat. The left-hand bank of the river here was surveyed, in 1805, by H. Bradley, Jr.[213] The right-hand bank was surveyed, in 1807, by Daniel Sullivan.[214] The "Buffalo trace" crossed White river at this point, hence the ferry right may have been valuable.[215]

A pioneer, probably N. Harlan, had settled on the bank of the river, and his possessions were surveyed and recorded as "Claim No. 3." [216] He was there before the land was divided into sections, so the surveyors made a special survey of his land and called it "Claim No. 3." He had land on both sides of the river. Many think Abraham Lincoln crossed White river at this ferry, in 1830, on his way to Illinois. It is perhaps the oldest ferry on White river, for it was at the

102

212 Histories of Gibson county, and Indiana Historical Society's Publications, Volume 2, pp. 359-365.

213 Record IX, *North and West*, pp. 403-406.

214 Record IX, *North and West*, p. 409.

215 Plat Book V, p. 157.

216 Record IX, pp. 411-425.

place the buffaloes crossed, and thousands of pioneers followed the "Buffalo trail," subsequently called "Buffalo trace," before other overland roads were cut out from Cincinnati and Louisville to Vincennes. There was a ferry near Petersburg, Indiana,[217] before 1798. It was operated by a Mr. Morrison, later of Aurora, Indiana.

SUPPOSED COPPER MINE.

In submitting an Indian treaty for ratification, on December 10, 1809, General William Henry Harrison wrote the government: "This small tract of about twenty miles square) is one of the most beautiful that can be conceived, and is moreover, believed to contain a very rich copper mine. I have, myself, frequently seen specimens of the copper; one of which I sent to Mr. Jefferson, in 1802. The Indians were so extremely jealous of any search being made for this mine that the traders were always cautioned not to approach the hills, which are supposed to contain the mine."[218] The treaty was signed December 9, 1809, and pertains to lands on the Wabash and Vermillion rivers, being in a direct line 20 miles from the mouth of the Vermillion river.

In 1793, George Inlay, a traveler wrote: "The copper mine on the Wabash is, perhaps the richest vein of copper in the bowels of the whole earth."[219] Of course, that is a

103

[217] Plat Book V, pp. 157-161; Record 9, *North and West*, pp. 403-406 and 411; Indiana Historical Society's Publications, Volume 2, p. 366, under *Sketch of Samuel Morrison.*

[218] *Early Travels in Indiana*, pp. 11, 129, 221, 28 and 38; American State Papers, Class II, *Indian Affairs*, p. 762; Indiana Historical Society's Publications, Volume 6, p. 319.

[219] *Early Travels in Indiana*, p. 11.

dream. In 1817, the Indians brought one lump of copper that weighed 28 pounds to Fort Harrison. It is supposed that the Indians found it about thirty miles above the mouth of Raccoon creek. These pieces were probably scattered on the surface and were brought down from the south shore of Lake Superior by glacial drifts.[220]

WILD PIGEON ROOST.

At the half-section corner between sections 16 and 17, township 3, south range 5 west, in Cass township, in Dubois county, the surveyors found a wild pigeon roost. The forest trees were stripped of their branches by the weight of the birds, and the ground was covered with pigeon excrement.[221] The official record reads: "Is a pigeon roost where the ground is covered with dung and the trees generally stripped of their branches." [222]

EAST FORK OF WHITE RIVER SURVEYED ON ICE.
(DRIFTWOOD FORK.)

Between Dubois, Daviess and Martin counties the meanderings of White river were taken on the ice, January 24, 1805, by Surveyor David Sandford. He refers to High Rock, in Daviess county, near the line of ranges 5 and 6, as "a remark-

220 *Early Travels in Indiana,* pp. 93 and 129; *The Dunes in Northern Indiana,* State Geologist's Reports, 1918, Indiana; Brown's *Western Gazetteer,* p. 80.

221 Record V, *South and West,* pp. 56-70, State Auditor's Office.

222 *Early Travels in Indiana,* pp. 49, 278, 316, 337, 456, 510 and 521; Wilson's *History of Dubois County,* p. 81; Indiana Historical Society's Publications, Volume 1, p. 53; Volume 5, p. 317.

able ledge of rocks on the north bank" [of White river].
His initials "D. S." are cut in this rock.

David Sandford was a native of Newtown, Connecticut,
and graduated from Yale in 1804, and in 1805 sub-divided
range 5, of the Vincennes tract, through what are now Dubois, Daviess and Martin counties. He also had a contract
to survey a reserve of four townships at the foot of the
rapids of the Maumee river, but took sick at Fort Wayne and
died there, Friday, October 11, 1805. He was buried the
same day at sunset. The writer has re-surveyed many of his
lines in range 5, and bears testimony to the young surveyor's
efficiency. Sandford [Sanford] was a careful surveyor and
left copious field notes. He was about twenty-five when he
died.[223]

Navigable rivers had to be surveyed. Smaller rivers were
measured in as land. The legislature appointed Surveyor
Alexander Ralston to survey the west fork of White river,
in 1825.

LILIES RETARD SURVEY.

In October, 1823, while making a survey of a tract 10 miles
square opposite the river A'boite, (on Little river south)
[Fort Wayne] Price F. Kellogg, the surveyor, found "an
impassable lily pond," and had to offset 6½ chains to get by
it.[224]

[223] Indiana Historical Society's Publication, Volume 2, pp. 359 and
360; Wilson's *History of Dubois County,* pp. 88-98; Indiana Historical
Society's Publications, Volume 5, p. 62; *Early Travels in Indiana,* p.
62; Brown's *Western Gazetteer,* 1817, p. 38-40.
[224] Miscellaneous Record I, p. 233.

MARBLE QUARRY.

There is a record of a "quarry of stone resembling marble," in Plat Book 1, page 99. The quarry is located about 3 miles east of Dupoint, in Jefferson county.

SURVEYORS IN DANGER.

In Cockrum's Pioneer History of Indiana mention is made of surveyors having trouble with the Indians. In the record of the survey of range IX, north and west, page 401, this entry appears: "Continued by Daniel Sullivan," which indicates the survey might have been suddenly suspended.

106

SWEARING IN CHAIN-CARRIER.

While surveying in township 2, range 1 west, not far from French Lick, Surveyor Arthur Henri found it necessary to swear in a new chain-carrier. His oath is written in the field notes, and reads as follows:

"I, James Ireland, do solemnly swear in the presence of Almighty God that in all measurements and surveys in which I shall be employed as chain-carrier, I will faithfully and impartially execute the trust reposed in me, so help me God."

His

"JAMES X IRELAND.

Mark

"Sworn and subscribed to before me, this 27th day of August, 1806.[225]

ARTHUR HENRI, D. S."

---

225 Record I, *North and West*. p. 61.

Base Line Cave in Orange County.

On the Base Line 370 feet west of the southeast corner of township 1, north range 2 west, about 6 miles east of the west line of Orange county, and about 6 or 7 miles southeast of French Lick, Ebenezer Buckingham, Jr., who surveyed the base line, found a remarkable cave. He says: "A remarkable cave, mouth about 30 feet in diameter. This cave descends perpendicular about 40 feet, then continues southeast about 6 rods, then out at the side of a hill.[226] October 15, 1804.

"Anderson's River."

In the field notes of Perry county, 1805, Anderson river, over which Abraham Lincoln conducted a ferry several years later, was referred to as "Anderson's river."[227]

Shield's Trading House.

At Seymour, Indiana, near the southeast corner of section 7, the surveyor's field notes show an improvement in 1807-1809, extending into sections 8 and 18, and marked "Improvements, Shield's Trading House." A drawing shows the "house." It was between the Grouseland treaty line and White river.[228]

[226] Volume II, *North and West*, p. 77.

[227] *Venable's Footprints of the Pioneers*, p. 108; Volume III, *South and West*, p. 119; Indiana Historical Society's Publications, Volume 6, Map, p. 296-7; *Early Travels in Indiana*, pp. 137, 213 and 270; *The Western Gazetteer* by Samuel R. Brown, p. 37.

[228] Plat Book I, p. 127.

Surveyor Discovers Coal in Dubois County.

West between sections 23 and 26, in township 1 north, range 5 west, appears this record: 62.20 chains from the southeast corner of section 23, township 1 north, range 5 west, "intersected left bank of White river; about 20 chains down the bank of the river from the place where this line meets the river there is a considerable stratum of excellent coal under a ledge of rocks that faces the river;[229] Tuesday, November 13, 1804. It was marked 'coal land.' "

Pioneer Expressions Used by Pioneer Surveyors.

The government surveyors described the land, etc., by such expressions as "wavely land," "gladly land," "somewhat gladly land," "middling soil," "sorry land," "low sloughy land," "run of a spring," "bed of a run," "brow of a hill." [230] Work was not always suspended on Sunday.

McDonald's Cabin and the Mudholes.

The surveyor's map in Plat Book V, page 27, shows the location of McDonald's cabin near the Mudholes, in Dubois county. He was the first settler in Dubois county. The Mudholes were often mentioned in General Harrison's military orders in territorial days. They were near the Buffalo trail,[231] at a point where the trail was crossed by a spur of

229 Volume V, *North and West*, p. 258.
230 Record V, *North and West,* on almost any page.
231 *Early Travels in Indiana,* p. 520.

the "Yellow Banks trail." Captain Dubois, after whom Dubois county was named, entered the land upon which the McDonald family had "squatted." "Yellow Banks" is now recognized as Owensboro, Kentucky.[232]

SHAWNEE TRACE.

This trace is technically located in the southeast corner of township 2 north, range 13 west, in Illinois, southwest of Vincennes.[233] It was a road from Vincennes to the south, and only incidentally connected with Indiana. The word Shawnee means "Southerner."

Space will not permit special mention in this paper of the surveys locating the state capital at Indianapolis, the Internal Improvement Surveys,[234] and other important surveys, the material facts relating to which have been included in various Indiana state and county histories, various historical papers, included in previous volumes of the publications of the Indiana Historical Society.

(Indianapolis, January 1, 1919.)

[232] Indiana Historical Society's Publications, Volume 6, pp. 290, 296 and 297.

[233] Plat Book II, p. 121; *Indiana and Indianans*, Volume 1, p. 95; *The Birkbeck Colony*.

[234] Indiana Historical Society's Publications, Volume 1, pp. 153, 154, 155; Volume 2, pp. 190, 191, 379 and 381; Volume 5, pp. 40, 41, 52, 62 and 158; Dr. Esarey's *Indiana*, Chapter XVI contains a splendid review of Improvement Surveys.

INDEX

Allen, Joseph A., (surveyor)	88
Allen, J. S., (surveyor)	87
Anderson, Indian Chief, grants Whetzell permission to cut trace	52
Bailey, John	58
Banks, Walter	52
Barber, Levi, (surveyor), early settler Perry County	11, 74
Base Line, established in Indiana	66, 70
Biggs, Uriah, (surveyor)	93
Birdseye, Indian trail near	11
Bloomington, Indian trails near	3
Blue River Trace, location and history	33-36
Boone, Squire	9
Bradley, H	102
Breckenridge, Alexander	58
Breckenridge, Robert	58
Bridgeton, Indian trail near	2
Brooks, Thomas J.	5, 6
Brownson, John, (surveyor)	4
Brownstown, Indian trail near	3
Buckingham, Ebenezer, (surveyor), early settler Perry County	11
makes original Indiana surveys	66-70
reports cave	107
Buffaloes, early existence in Indiana	20, 24
Buffalo Trace, location	1
Indian name	1, 21
survey of	1, 74-75
history and description	16-32
Buntin, R	102
Burnet, Judge Jacob	30
Burnet, Abraham, reserve for	89
Burnet, Isaac, reserve for	89
Burnet, James, reserve for	89
Burnet, Rebecca, reserve for	89
Burr, Aaron, in Indiana	32, 43
Campbell, John	58
Carlisle, Indian trail near	13
Carter, Chauncey, (surveyor)	88, 89
Clark, Gen. George Rogers, route of	12, 13, 22, 25, 36
grant to	57-61
Clark, William, (surveyor)	57, 58
Clark's Grant, survey of	57-61
Coalbank, in Indiana in 1804	108
Coppermine, reported in Indiana	103-104
Corydon, Indian trail to	9
Cotton, "Judge" William	5
Cravens, Joseph M.	30
Croghan, Col. George	22, 23
Croghan, William	57, 58
Cuzco, Rangers camp at	31

Dana, Indian trail near 3
Daniel, Capt. W. H. 43
Dearborn County, Indian trails in 4, 5
Dubois, Capt. Toussaint 49, 109
Dubois County, settlement movement 32
Elliott, Chester 92
Fleming, William 58
Foote, Dr. William 101, 102
Foote, Ziba 101, 102
Foote's Grave Pond, history of 100-102
Fort Harrison, map of 13; 90-91
Fort McDonald, at "The Mudholes" 11
    stopping place 20-21, 31
Fort William, (Carrolton, Ky.) 4
Foyles, ----, stage route 26
Freeman, Thomas, (surveyor) 5, 11, 12, 13, 14, 20, 47, 63-74
    sketch 66
Freeman's Corners 63-64
Fredonia, Indian trails at 36
French Lick, Indian trail near 5
    whetstone cave near 19
    springs at discovered by surveyor 99
    cave near 107
Fuquay, John, (scout) 37, 39, 43
Galloway, Peter S. 82
Goodnow, Samuel, (surveyor) 98
Gosport, Indian trail at 3, 14
Grigsbee, Sarah Lincoln, grave of 40
Grouseland Treaty Line, survey of 76
Gurney, Mrs., rescue of 28
Hanna, Samuel 92
Hargrove, Capt. William 29
    orders to 35, 39, 41, 45, 50
Harlan, N., Ferry of 2, 19, 27
Harlan's Ferry, on White River 102
Harmar, Col. Josiah, routes of 11, 24
Harris, William, (surveyor) 78, 80, 81, 83, 91
Harrison, Gen. William H, land purchase from Indians 1-4, 76-80
    mention of 7, 17, 31, 32, 35, 39, 41, 42, 45, 47, 49, 50, 51, 53
Harrison Purchase, location and survey 1-3, 76-80
Hay, Samuel 19, 36
Helm, Capt. Leonard 36
Henri, Arthur, surveys Grouseland purchase 76, 78, 106
Heth, Andrew 58
Hillsdale, Indian trail near 3
Hindostan (Townsite at falls on east fork of White River) established 5
    abandoned 7
Hodgson, John 82
Hogue, Sergeant 27
Howard, William 82
Howe, Thomas 52

Indiana, surveys of state lines   80-84
Indians, trails of   1-16
    object of Harrisons purchase   3
    town destroyed   36
    teacher for Delawares   37
    surveys of reservations for   85-91
    threaten surveyors   86-87, 106
Imlay, George, quoted   103-104
Ireland, James   106
Iron Ore, reported in Indiana   95
Kankakee, survey of swamp of   93-98
Kellogg, Price F., (surveyor)   89, 105
Kendricks, E. P., (surveyor)   80, 83
Kentucky, routes of immigrants from   8
    uncertain land titles in   65
Kibbey, Capt. E., cuts road   104-105
Kibbey's Road, location   4-5, 93
Larkins, -----, killed by Indians   29
Lawrenceburg, Indian trail near   5
Leopold, Indian trail near   9
Liberty, Indian trail near   4
Lincoln, Abraham, route of in Indiana   2, 30, 40-41, 65, 102
    ferry on Anderson's River   106
"Lincoln Way", established   31
Long Hair, Chief, reserve for   89
Loughery, Col. Archibald, defeat of   22
Ludlow, Israel   62
McClellan, Abraham   92
McDonald, John, (surveyor)   2-3
    surveys "Ten O'Clock Line"   77, 82, 92
McDonald, John   28-29, 32
McDonald, William   28-29, 32
Marble Quarry, reported   106
Metea, Indian Chief, reserve of   89
Miami National Reserve, survey of   85-88
Michigan Road, survey of   91-92
Miller, John   45, 48n
Montgomery, John   58
Moore, James   58
Morris, B. F., (surveyor)   8
Mounts, Mathias   26
Mudholes, the fort at   11
    buffaloes at   20, 21, 26, 27
    first settlement in Dubois County   28, 35, 41, 42, 108
Neely, John I.   92
New Albany, Indian trail near   7
Newburg, formerly Sprinkleburg   47
New Harmony, Indian trail from   11
Niblack, County Agent   44
Odon, Indian trails near   14
Orleans, Indian trail near   5

Patoka River, fords in 37, 40
   beavers in 42
   ferry on 45, 48n
Pigeon Roost, Indian trail at 7
   massacre at 33
Pigeons, numbers of 104
Pioneer Expressions, used by surveyors 108
Polk, William 92
Portersville, first county seat of Dubois County 5, 44
Pride, Woolsey 28
Princeton, Indian trail near 11
Raccoon Creek, beginning of "Ten O'Clock Line" 2-3, 77
Ralston, Gov. Samuel M. 30
Rangers, service in early Indiana 27-29
   camps 31-35
   orders to 35, 39, 41, 45, 50
Reaugh, Thomas 92
Rector, William, (surveyor), surveys Buffalo Trace 1-2, 75
   early settler Perry County 11
   mention 17, 101
Red Banks, (Henderson, Ky.) Indian trail from 8, 12
   location and history of trail 44-47
Rockport, sale of lots at 43
Rome, Indian trail from 8-10, 11
   called "Washington" 11
Rush, Richard 52
Rush, Thomas 52
Salt, manufacture of by early settlers 47-49
Salt Route 47-50
Sanford, David 105
St. Clair Arthur Jr. 30
Seek, Indian Chief, reserve of 89
Selvin, fort at 43
Settedown, Shawnee Chief 47
Severns, John 39, 48, 49-50
Shawnee Trace 12, 9
Shields Trading House, trail to 4, 5
Sibley, Sylvester, (surveyor) 82
Smith, Hosea 25
Smith, Jeremiah, (surveyor), quoted 95, 98
Springville, first county seat of Clark County 7
   stockade at 8
Sprinkles, Maj. John 45, 47
Squibb, Nathaniel L. 100
Stage Coaches, early line of in Indiana 26
Stone, Augustus 99
Sullivan, Daniel 102, 106
Surveyors, early instruments, clothing, etc. 70-71
   threatened by Indians 86-87, 106
   curious notes by 95-97, 99-109
Surveys, system in Indiana 55-57

113

of Clarks Grant   57-60
of Greenville treaty line   61-62
of Vincennes Tract   62-65
rectangular system introduced   66-72
of Buffalo Trace   74-75
of Grouseland treaty line   76
of "Ten O'Clock Line"   76-80
of state lines   80-84
of Indian reservations   84-91
of Fort Harrison   91
of Michigan road   91-92
of Kankakee swamps   93-98
incidental notes by   99-109
Taylor, Richard   58
Tecumseh, Shawnee Chief, objects to "Ten O'Clock Line"   3, 78-80
"Ten O'Clock Line", location and survey   2-3, 76-78
story of Indian objection   79-80
Terrill, Richard   58
Tevebaugh, George   26
Thorntown, Indian trail to   14
reserve surveyed   88
Tipton, John   27, 33, 35
Todd, Robert   58
Trails, general review of   1-16
map of   15
modern roads on   12, 14, 26-32
Trinity Springs, Indian trails near   14
Tupper, Edward W.   99
Vallonia, Indian trail from   7, 32-33
Vance, A. St. Clair, (surveyor)   87
Vincennes, Indian grant at   1-2
survey of   62-74
Indian trails to   3, 14
governed state line   81, 83
Vincennes Tract, survey of   2, 63-74
origin of   62
settlement of   65
Waverly, road to cut   51, 53
Weik, Jesse W.   30
West Baden, springs at discovered by surveyors   99-100
Whetzell, Cyrus, sketch   52-53
Whetzell, Jacob, cuts trace to White River   51, 53
Whetzell's Trace, location and history   51-53
White River, east fork called "Driftwood" or "Muddy Fork"   8, 26
road to west fork cut   51-53
partial survey on ice   104
Williams, M. F., (surveyor-general)   82
Wilson, George B., erects monument at Mudholes   31-32
Yellow Banks, (Owensboro, Ky.), Indian trail from   8, 11
marker on   31
location and history of trail   36, 44